MORMON CHRONICLES
of Deception

A Personal Journey of Biblical Truth

By Tom Hall

Kenu Foundation Publishing
Second Edition

MORMON CHRONICLES
of Deception

A Personal Journey of Biblical Truth

Published by:
Kenu Foundation Publishing
Waukesha, Wisconsin, U.S.A.
Printed in U.S.A.

Scripture is from the Holy Bible, New King James Version
Copyright 1982 by Thomas Nelson, Inc.

Library of Contress Cataloging-in-Publication Data
Hall, Tom
Mormon Chronicles of Deception

ISBN 978-0-939497-27-0
Second Edition 2008

Dedication

To my loving wife, Jacque, and our children…

God's blessing to us:

Tom, Kerri, and David

Foreword

Having found salvation in Christ at a Billy Graham Crusade, one of the first things I was moved to do was to write to him, sharing my experiences.

After thanking him for his influence in my life as a teenager, I shared my experience in Mormonism and how God had faithfully led me back into His way again. I sent him a copy of a tract I had written in my efforts to reach Mormons still unaware of the contradictions between the Bible and the Mormon doctrines.

I even shared the loss of my family with him and how the joys of my faith in Christ outweighed the suffering I had endured. I had read Billy Graham's book entitled, *Approaching Hoofbeats*, and I knew that he was well informed on the cults and vitally interested in seeing to it that people come to know the truth. I assured him of my support and prayers in his ministry.

My heart was lifted by a response that came to me from his office, written by E.M. Engman. Among other things, it said:

> *"Mr. Graham appreciates learning of your early experience of attending the first crusade to be held and of your making your commitment to Christ in Henrietta Mears' Bible class. We rejoice that the Lord was faithful and enlightened your understanding about Mormonism, bringing you out of that cult. Surely losing your wife, family and friends must have been very difficult for you, but we do praise God that you had the courage to follow His leading, and you now feel that God is directing your life. May God bless you and prosper your ministry to others who have been deceived by Mormonism."*

With such encouragement, building a new life in Christ has been a wonderful experience.

Tom Hall

Table of Contents

CHAPTER ONE

Early Impressions

The first crusade that Billy Graham held was in Los Angeles at the corner of Washington and Hill Streets. Although I was only a teenager, the crusade influenced my life far beyond anything that I understood at the time. As a matter of fact, I thought it had been of little influence because I didn't become "religious."

Of greater impact was my attendance at Hollywood Presbyterian Church where I was part of a Bible study class taught by Henrietta Mears. I liked being there and wanted to take part more than I did. It seemed to me that I would need seminary training to hold down anything more than a spot in the choir. I contented myself with that and my life went on, but I drifted away from the church.

My detour into Mormonism began in a Hollywood restaurant where two fellow salesmen and I gathered after a routine day as advertising representatives. As we lounged around our table, we couldn't help noticing the attractive young lady across the room. I was so taken, I couldn't keep my eyes off her, even though she was with a young man. My friends began to challenge me to use my selling skills to get her phone number. I lost my nerve, but one of the others decided to use his "superior" ability, and he got the number for me!

The next day was as long as I could wait to phone Jennifer. It didn't surprise me to find out that she was a model on a popular TV show. She would go out with me! The next two weeks seemed like a miracle of God's direction. We had three dates during which she challenged me to read *The Book of Mormon*, introduced me to Ellis Craig (a Mormon missionary who invited me to have six introductory church lessons), and The Church of Jesus Christ of Latter-Day Saints (LDS) leadership recruited me to serve as Activity Director for the Young Adults Mutual Improvement Association! I was flattered beyond measure, and pride filled my heart to think that I was important to so many nice people.

1

I was really glad that all this encouragement and attention had finally brought me to the place where I had good reason to quit smoking. I'd been trying to rid myself of this addiction for several years, but with the instruction I was getting and the support of the people in this church, I won the battle.

I was impressed with the assertion that their church, The Church of Jesus Christ of Latter-Day Saints, offered me a lifestyle that would seem to raise me to new heights of spirituality and good works. Ellis had become my spiritual mentor and I was baptized a Mormon, totally unaware that I had been taken in by a cult which would one day attempt to destroy my life as it had been, robbing me of my family and all I held dear.

Meanwhile, a serious relationship with my gorgeous girlfriend was all that mattered. I was crazy about her, and she seemed to be equally in love with me. My spiritual side was also being challenged with this new "disciplined" Mormon way of life, while my heart was being swept away by the squeaky-clean image of Jennifer. My emotions had never reacted with such positive feelings about such a seemingly perfect young woman.

Because of this, it came as a shock when less than a month into our relationship, Jennie announced somewhat matter-of-factly that we had to stop dating since she was engaged to be married! Her fiancé's job had kept our paths from crossing since he worked nights and I worked days.

However, even while under her spell, I hadn't failed to notice that there were any number of lovely girls in the church. It was even true that several of them had made some advances which had also inflated my ego to the bursting point.

By then, I had also quit drinking alcoholic beverages, tea and Cokes in pursuit of Joseph Smith's "revealed" law of health known as The Word of Wisdom. For me, my new accomplishments seemed miraculous. It felt great to be an integral part of my new "family," taking some leadership, learning about my "eternal progression" in the missionary lessons and finding new friends who referred to me as "Brother Hall" and were intensely committed to my successful integration into the Mormon Church. Where had this church been all my life?

It was no time before I had fallen for another talented and beautiful Mormon girl. Vivacious and confident, she also seemed to epitomize the positive personal growth of the ideal Latter-Day Saint. By the time Ellis had taken me through the several weeks of missionary lessons, I could not have been more impressed with the love and attention shown to me by so many members of the church. He said he knew God had led me to the "only true church of Jesus Christ" in the world today. He wanted me to fully experience the wonderful blessings of membership in "**The** Church."

I accepted Ellis's insistent persuasion as Godly-inspired evangelism. It also occurred to me that he had spent so much time fellowshipping me, I felt obligated to him to accept his challenge to be baptized by immersion. After all, it seemed I had everything to gain and nothing to lose.

Wasn't he just sharing a **restored** gospel that was apparently needed to counter all the various Christian denominations with their man-made doctrines?

Wasn't it possible for God **to reveal** His will to His prophets as in times past? It just seemed like everyone I met in the church was reaching out to me with so much love and attention.

Shouldn't I be thinking about settling down? Wasn't it proof of God's love for me to have a church "family" that referred to me as "Brother Hall"? These were such goal-oriented, hard-working people. They really stimulated my interest in learning more about their purposeful lives.

I trusted in this **new gospel** message that sounded so perfect and seemed to fulfill all my needs. Mormons appeared to have an ordered discipline that I had never found in other churches. This new way of life seemed able to release me from my bad habits (hadn't I even quit smoking?), and to help me rise above Satan's temptations. I felt both smug and pious, so much so that I called Hollywood Presbyterian Church to inform them of my newfound revelation. The sadness I heard in the pastor's voice was incomprehensible to me then. I gave little thought to his question, "Do you really know what you're getting into, Tom?"

There were to be many years from my baptism as a Mormon to my authentic Christian re-baptism, but God had planted the seed of His Word in my heart that eventually made life as a Mormon impossible for me. I had heard the Gospel from Billy Graham. I had learned to accept the Bible as God's Word from Henrietta Mears. Even with layer upon layer of Mormon doctrine burying the truth in my heart, it was as irrepressible as the tiny seed hidden in the warm soil of spring. As spring rains come, it cannot help but grow. If there is a rock on top, the seedling grows around it, seeking the sun. If a branch is broken off, the seedling sprouts six new branches in its place. The truth that was buried in my heart would not die or fade away. Beyond that, the Lord Jesus, Himself, sustained me in all the difficult decisions I had to make in leaving the LDS Church.

This buried truth went unrecognized while revealing itself in various ways. An illustration of this happened one evening when my new girlfriend and I went to a leadership meeting at an LDS Church at Adams and Figueroa, a black neighborhood. This particular Mormon Church had been one of the first in Los Angeles, and when it was founded, it was in a white neighborhood. As the area deteriorated, it became a much smaller white church in a black neighborhood. Amazingly, there was not one black member in attendance.

I verbalized this observation to the group of young people there and the answer came in a chorus! Almost in unison, they said that President David O. McKay alone could know "God's plan for the Negro." There were some blacks in the church...somewhere...but since they couldn't hold the priesthood, few of them were interested in joining. Inwardly, I saw a question mark rise out of the floor and hang suspended in the forefront of my mind. Outwardly, I just said, "Oh."

This question was lost in the days that followed, and my latest "dream girl" and I found ourselves involved in many church activities of common interest. Together, we enjoyed leadership positions in an LDS theatrical group. Our lives were church-oriented and both of us found opportunity to express and enlarge our acting talents there. Eventually, these shared experiences led to a deepening relationship. I was thrilled when she agreed to marry me; however, this was to be a "celestial marriage" only after I had progressed to a point of "worthiness" and had achieved the priesthood level of an elder.

My motivation was a supreme appointment to meet God's requirements for perfection! The bishop was my coach, and within a year we were making plans for our wedding in full temple regalia. It was to be a noble achievement demanding dedicated effort. I was so proud of the steps I had taken to rise above the commonplace and be a part of this select level of Latter-Day Saints. It was an accomplishment reserved for those who pursued total perfection by their works of righteousness, and I thought I had finally reached this first step toward personal exaltation!

The day of our wedding arrived! As part of the day's activity, there was a two-hour ceremony in which I was expected to "take out my own endowments." At one point, I was given the option of leaving if I did not care to participate; however, it was obvious to me that there would be no wedding to follow if I left at that moment. I was required to take a "blood"[1] oath in the course of this bizarre ceremony, and in spite of my strong misgivings, I proceeded under the pressure of the moment. No opportunity had been given me to consider these commitments since I had never been advised ahead of time what would be expected of me. The reason given for not informing me was that "sacred" ordinances could not be revealed outside the temple walls!

After the two-hour temple "endowment," our wedding lasted just about fifteen minutes. The vows were to the effect that we were being married for "time and all eternity" with the possibility of becoming a god and goddess. There was no mention of a personal relationship with Jesus Christ - only the words at the close of prayers, "In the name of Jesus Christ." That seemed inconsistent with the pronouncements of doom I heard in the ceremony if I failed to live up to each and every oath to which I swore. The weddings I had attended at Hollywood Presbyterian Church had honored Christ alone as the head of the newly-formed home. I had expected our wedding to be similar, and I took note of this omission with considerable discomfort. It was also sad that my parents (non-Mormons) were not permitted to attend the wedding. Only if they had agreed to become "worthy" church members, could they have attended the ceremony.

---

[1] A symbolic gesture

For the next sixteen years, I threw myself into priesthood responsibilities, leading the choir, directing dramas, doing home visitation, teaching Sunday School and attending innumerable meetings, meetings and more meetings! There were times even with so many church-related activities, that I wondered why Jesus no longer had any significance as Lord and Savior. And it wasn't just me! No one ever testified about knowing Jesus or having Him as a personal, indwelling part of his or her life - not even at the monthly fast and testimony meetings. When He was mentioned, it was as though He were a superficial ingredient for our spiritual lives since becoming perfect in good works is the essence of Mormonism.

Instead, Mormon testimonies usually began, "I know the church is true. I know Joseph Smith was a prophet of God and I know the Book of Mormon is true." Like the rest of them, my life gave the outward appearance of order and discipline - conformity to rules and regulations. In my heart, however, I knew that it was a different story. Well camouflaged, my sinful nature was alive and well, no matter how things looked from the outside. Guilt was my constant companion.

My Mormon marriage was built on a foundation of mutual interests and dedication to the LDS Church system. We both anticipated having a large family - the larger, the better! After the birth of our first son, Tom, the joys of parenthood were beyond imagination, inseparably connected with our church responsibilities as parents.

Our divine appointment was predicated on the challenge of having as many children as possible and we didn't need encouragement to enlarge our family.

> "No parent can escape that obligation and that responsibility...
> Legions of choice spirits are waiting for their tabernacles
> of flesh to progress to their God-planned destiny"
> (Conference Report, October 12, 1942, p. 12).

Our plans for a large family were side-tracked, however. We were blessed to join the ranks of parents chosen by God to raise two very special children - children afflicted with cerebral palsy.

In complete agreement and after much trepidation, my wife and I made a mutual commitment to keep Dougie and Patti in our home as long as possible. Without my realizing it, the Lord had given us a strength I never imagined possible. For the next twelve years, our lives were enveloped in the unrelenting routine of caring for our "Angels Unaware." In my need, Dale Evans' book by that name began to influence me to lean on His everlasting arms, and not on my own.

I kept looking to "The Church" to provide answers to the unanswerable. Slowly but surely, church work lost its importance to me. My heart was desperately reaching out for the spiritual food that I wasn't getting in the LDS Third Ward.

"Why me, Lord?" Why wasn't our family measuring up to the "perfectionism" that Mormon families always seemed to achieve?

I still clung to the Church, seeking spiritual answers for the intense frustration we faced with our severely handicapped children at home. Doctors had continually urged us to place them in a state hospital, but we were filled with the instinct to nurture and love them ourselves, devoting our lives to meeting their needs at home as long as we were able to do so.

I was struggling to find spiritual direction from our church leaders and the ward bishop to no avail. No one was able to counsel us on how to help our oldest son, Tom, deal with the problems he was having just coping with the adjustments he needed to make.

I now believe that my handicapped children had become the catalyst for many of my emerging convictions. I was becoming more and more tolerant of individual differences. I learned to accept my students without prejudice since I was teaching in a somewhat disadvantaged area. As I looked into the faces of several black students, still burdened with the scars of discrimination, and saw genuine people with real feelings and dreams, I thought many times of the words in Matthew 25:40 where Jesus said,

> *"Inasmuch as ye have done it unto (that is, cared for) these,*
> *my brethren, ye have done it unto me."*

My heart went out to these young people. Through no fault of their own, they were not receiving the help and encouragement in life that they needed. I felt a sudden responsibility to reach out to them with a love I had never experienced in all of the sixteen years I had been a Mormon. The darkness of their skin became a light to my faltering Mormon ego. God began to reveal Himself to me as never before.

One evening, the bishop called me into his office to say that one of my students had decided to join our church. He thanked me for giving his name to the missionaries and said the boy was very interested in knowing more about Mormonism. The bishop then suggested that my position as a teacher would make it possible for me to do a lot more of this kind of work. In view of all this, he called me to an even higher position, a priesthood office called a "Seventy." I now had the opportunity to become a part-time missionary right there in my own home town! I was interested about the possibilities! Perhaps I would find solace in leading others to "The Church."

CHAPTER TWO

Prophecies or Policies?

As a Mormon, I could see the missionary advantage of my status as a high school teacher, but I had some reservations that caused me to return to the question I had asked so many years before.

At the white LDS church within the black community boundaries of Los Angeles, I had asked, "What about blacks?" A number of my students were blacks and I felt that if anyone needed what the church could provide, it was those kids! That was in 1975. Integration was the law of the land, yet my church had been practicing discrimination against blacks since the early 1800s.

> "The negroes are not equal with other races where the receipt of certain spiritual blessings are concerned, particularly the priesthood and the temple blessings that flow therefrom, but this inequality is not of man's origin. It is the Lord's doing, based on His eternal laws of justice..." (*Mormon Doctrine*, 10th printing, pp. 527-8).

What "eternal laws of justice?" Was it the degree of darkness of their skin? It seemed ridiculous to me to try to justify a church policy by just saying it was the "Lord's doing" without any biblical reference. Was it really "the Lord's doing?" Which of "His eternal laws of justice" had blacks violated to bring this judgment upon themselves?

Something in me made me want to challenge the church on this point. I reasoned that some of the people of India are quite dark skinned. Would they be denied the priesthood too, even though they were not negroid? I wrote to S. Dilworth Young, the highest church missionary authority, about India. Since it was actually blacks I was curious about, I couldn't have expected a more blatant admission of prejudice by a church leader.

July 25, 1975
Mr. T.W. Hall
Re: Missionary Work in India

Dear Brother Hall:

Thank you for your recent letter concerning the above named subject.

We have had missionaries working in India in the last three years; but because of visa and other political problems, they have been withdrawn.

We are working to have our missionaries labor in every part of the world; and the only reason that they are not in certain countries is because of these visa problems or, as in the case of many countries in Africa, *the population is made up of mostly negroes.*

Thank you again for writing.
Sincerely your brethren,

THE FIRST COUNCIL OF THE SEVENTY
By S. Dilworth Young

The LDS Church had more full-time missionaries than any other denomination, and they used Matthew 28:19 liberally, proclaiming the high calling of going to "all nations to preach the Gospel." Besides, that was a verse I had learned well at Hollywood Presbyterian Church. I knew that it was part of the Bible, and I believed it. Yet, here in his letter, the highest Mormon missionary leader said that blacks were not being evangelized, nor would they be, simply because they were black!

In my search for biblical truth, I discovered, *"prove all things, holding fast to that which is good…"* (I Thess. 5:21). Now, I was faced with an undeniable contradiction between the church and God's Word, the Bible. Still, I sought some explanation of the church's position in this matter. I went to the highest priesthood authority in our area. He was a close friend and I felt I could lay the problem out before him and talk about it.

President Brown said that he disagreed with church policy in this matter too. He said that the whole thing was not doctrinal but a traditional policy of the church. He also gave me an independently published magazine called, *Dialogue*, which was designed to be a public forum for critical thinking and re-thinking of church policy.

I came to understand that mine weren't the first questions on this subject. Many others questioned discrimination of blacks as well as other policies of the church. Slowly, it dawned on me that the church was not the perfect institution I had believed it to be.

President Brown's counsel was that, although this was a controversial issue, it would be foolish for me to give up all of the excellent programs of the church over a single question. It was rather irrelevant as far as he was concerned.

Too late! All those things I had learned from the Bible through the years came pecking their way back into my mind. Whether it applied to my life or not, the importance of the issues was what the Bible had to say about it. I was not the criterion; the Bible was. Suddenly, I was quoting Bible verses to him that showed that all men are equal in God's sight; God is no respecter of persons; in Christ there is no difference between people. As I struggled to convey my discoveries to him, I said things that indicated my unwillingness to let it go. I also intimated that such bigotry made me ashamed to call myself a Mormon.

President Brown assured me that the time would come when blacks would be accepted. In the meantime, he warned me not to "throw the baby out with the bath water." His answers fell far short of satisfying me. On the contrary, just in leafing through my Bible, I found verse after verse that shored up my conviction that this teaching was anti-Christian. I learned how to use a concordance and I found even more verses such as Matthew 24:14:

> *"This gospel of the kingdom shall be preached in all the world for a witness unto all nations."*
>
> *God is not one to show partiality, but in every nation the man who fears Him and does what is right is welcome to Him"* (Acts 10:34,35).
>
> *"There is neither Jew nor Greek, there is neither slave nor free, there is neither male nor female; for you are all one in Christ Jesus"* (Gal. 3:28).
>
> *"Go ye...and teach all nations..."* (Matt. 28:19).

- Before my conversion to Mormonism, I had accepted the Bible as God's authoritative Word.
- Billy Graham had used the Bible as the highest authority given among men.
- Henrietta Mears had taught the value of accepting God's Word at face value.
- To ignore the fact that Mormon doctrine contradicted God's Word would be a whole lot more than "throwing the baby out with the bath water!"

For five months, I lived in a state of denial. I knew the problem. I could see the contradiction. I wanted to believe that "all was well in Zion," but I knew it wasn't. Five months of this hypocrisy was all I could stand.

I wouldn't allow myself to consider the personal cost that might be involved. I wrote my first, but it was not to be my last, doctrinal protest to a Mormon authority. This time, I didn't talk about India. I wrote about the black students who sat in my classrooms and what I thought was their need for the teachings of the church. Here is my letter:

December 30, 1975

S. Dilworth Young
First Council of the Seventy
Salt Lake City, Utah

Dear Brother Young:

Having been ordained to the role of a Seventy in the Third Ward, I have felt privileged to serve the Lord in this capacity. Through this calling I have become more aware of the great responsibility inherent with preaching the gospel, but I have become frustrated in my desire to be dedicated to this church service. As a high school English teacher, it has been rewarding to have been responsible for bringing our church into the lives of a number of my students, but I also feel hypocritical and discriminatory when I look into the eyes of the black students who need our church program more than perhaps any other ethnic group I come in contact with.

I have sought an answer to this dilemma, but no one can really give me an answer that makes sense. Hopefully, you will be able to clarify the discrepancies that exist between what the Scriptures state and the stand our church makes evident through the example stated in your letter.

The Scriptures I refer to are Mark 16:15 (*"go...and preach the gospel to every creature"*) and Colossians 1:23. Also Matthew 28:19 (*"...teach all nations"*), but the most emphatic to me is from Matthew 25:40 which says *"Verily I say unto you, inasmuch as ye have done it to one of the least of these, ye have done it unto Me."*

When I received your letter stating that Africa was out of bounds to missionary work, it struck me like a bolt of lightning that our doctrine of discrimination against blacks is one of the most bigoted and unrealistic attitudes I can imagine. Our church has far too much to offer to exclude any human race. I write these things for the love of the gospel and in the name of Jesus Christ.

Sincerely,
Thomas W. Hall

No answer. Three months passed and still no response. Every weekday, I faced those black students with their questioning eyes and felt compelled to find an answer for them. They didn't know what they needed, but I did. Why should they be denied what I considered to be God's truth?

Finally I could wait no longer, so I called President Young's office in Salt Lake City. It was a shock to hear his voice at the other end of the line! He had answered the phone directly! We exchanged greetings and then I asked him about my letter. He claimed he never received it, so I could do no less than immediately read my copy of the letter to him on the phone right then!

His silent indignation at my words, "bigotry and discrimination," came over the telephone wire very plainly. His breathing was audible and when he spoke, his tone of voice became very stern. He promised to answer and to send information that clear up the matter "once and for all." He sent the following letter, and it did indeed clear up the matter for me:

The Church of Jesus Christ of Latter-Day Saints
The Council of the Seventy
47 E. South Temple Street
Salt Lake City, Utah

April 7, 1976

Dear Brother Hall:

You want some material on the Church's stand on Negroes. While there is nothing official, a man by the name of Stewart has compiled several statements by the president of the Church. If you will write to the Deseret Book Company asking for the book Brother Stewart wrote about the Negroes, you will be sent some information. It is a small book and does not cost very much.

The policy of the Church is as has been stated. We do not give the priesthood to Negroes. This is the policy of the First Presidency who we uphold as prophets, seers, and revelators. I suppose you will have to make a choice as to whether or not you want to recognize President Kimball as a prophet, seer, or revelator. If you do, this question will not bother you anymore.

Sincerely yours,
S. Dilworth Young

In my thinking, he had stated it succinctly: I either had to accept President Kimball's dictates as "prophet, seer, and revelator," or believe God's Word as recorded in the Bible - the choice was not difficult.

CHAPTER THREE

To Make a Choice

President Young's ultimatum was unequivocal: Mormon leadership - accept it or reject it. My mind went back through the years to my early teaching which placed the Bible as a Christian's ultimate authority and Jesus as personal Lord and Savior. Fleeting thoughts reminded me of the fact that I had heard nothing about knowing Jesus in a personal relationship during my years in the Mormon Church.

Didn't the Church make Jesus "Lord of lords and King of kings?" Was not God the "only Lord and God?" I had always thought that is what the Church stood for. How then could they hold to a doctrine so clearly in contradiction to what the Bible teaches? What was more, President Young was asking me to accept what the Church teaches and to ignore what the Bible says. According to him, the goal seemed to be that I reach a place where I no longer questioned the Church and its teachings.

All those years before when I asked Jesus to come into my heart and save me, He had indeed moved into my life. However, I really couldn't call Him Lord simply because I had never studied His Word in any depth. He was there in spite of my lack of acknowledgement of His presence. He had not left me, and now He would no longer allow me to tolerate Mormon teaching, nor would He allow me to ignore biblical authority. Although I had been ignorant concerning biblical Christianity, He was faithful to me. My unquestioning belief in the Bible instilled in me the expectation that Mormon spiritual leaders would also believe it and align themselves with the clear teachings of Scripture.

Even so, I could not make such a monumental decision without further investigation. I went to an evangelical Christian church in downtown Glendale the next Sunday. The members there didn't know me or the turmoil going on in my life; and I was glad they didn't because I wanted to find God's answer without any outside pressure.

The pastor preached from the first chapter of Hebrews. His topic was the believer's need to rely solely on Jesus.

"In times past, God spoke to man through the prophets. In these last days, He speaks to us through His Son" (Heb. 1: 1,2).

Yet for eighteen years, I had been taught by the Mormon Church that the current "living prophet" of that Church was God's communicator to His people.

I looked back at the simple words of Scripture: "God spoke to prophets in times past ... in these last days, God speaks through His Son." I could hear God speaking to me personally and directly that morning. All intermediaries were gone and I heard God's Word and the Holy Spirit in my heart with my spiritual ears. They were in complete agreement! No "prophet" knew about it nor did anyone act on my behalf. It was pure spring water to my parched soul.

President Young had told me either to choose to uphold President Kimball as a prophet, seer and revelator...or not.

This was no light matter since I had finally turned to the Bible for my truly authoritative answers. I searched the Scriptures diligently only to find again and again that Jesus is presented as the fulfillment of the Old Testament prophets (Matt. 5:17) and He is the *"Chief Cornerstone"* of our faith (Matt. 21:42).

The more I read of God's Word, the less I could accept Mormon teaching. Priesthood authority was unfounded, and if the Church was so blatantly wrong about that (one of its foundational teachings), they might also be wrong on other things. On the other hand, I could find no fault in the Bible presentation of Jesus. The Bible has stood the test of time and assault from critics and unbelievers. Throughout the centuries, millions of people have found comfort and strength to live by in its pages.

The Christian church has taken many forms, but it has survived the greatest test of all differences within. People who believe the Bible may carry many names, but there has been a great unity among them based on their acceptance of Scripture as God's authoritative Word. Always, Jesus has been the center and head of the Christian church. There was no revelation that prophets alone were to give leadership and direction to His church.

I was thrilled to contemplate that I could approach God's Throne directly and no longer walk in the shadow of any Mormon prophet.

Here is an article by Ezra Taft Benson outlining the functions of the Mormon prophets:

> MORMON PROPHET President Ezra Taft Benson; Brigham Young University Devotional Assembly; Tuesday, February 26, 1980, 10:00 a.m.
>
> ...In conclusion let us summarize this grand key, these "Fourteen Fundamentals in Following the Prophet," for our salvation hangs on them.

FIRST:	The prophet is the only man who speaks for the Lord in everything.
SECOND:	The living prophet is more vital to us than the standard works. (Including the Bible!)
THIRD:	The living prophet is more important to us than a dead prophet.
FOURTH:	The prophet will never lead the Church astray.
FIFTH:	The prophet is not required to have any particular training or credentials to speak on any subject or act on any matter at any time.
SIXTH:	The prophet does not have to say, "Thus Saith the Lord," to give us scripture.
SEVENTH:	The prophet tells us what we need to know, not always what we want to know.
EIGHTH:	The prophet is not limited by men's reasoning.
NINTH:	The prophet can receive revelation on any matter, temporal or spiritual.
TENTH:	The prophet may be involved in civic matters.
ELEVENTH:	Two groups who have the greatest difficulty following the prophet are the proud who are learned and the proud who are rich.
TWELFTH:	The prophet will not necessarily be popular with the world or the worldly.

| THIRTEENTH: | The prophet and his counselor make up the first Presidency - the highest quorum in the Church. |
| FOURTEENTH: | The prophet and the presidency - the living prophet and the First Presidency - follow them and be blessed - reject them and suffer. |

While Mr. Benson says that "The prophet is the ONLY man who speaks for the Lord," the Bible says that *"There is one God and one Mediator between God and men, the Man Christ Jesus"* (I Tim. 2:5). Point after point of Mr. Benson's list is completely the opposite of the Bible's statements on the matter. I searched through Galatians 1:6-8 and 10, Matthew 7:15 and 24:24, and John 15:5 only to be more convinced than ever that I must believe what the Bible says.

The LDS teacher's manual says,

> "Any Latter-Day Saint who denounces or opposes, whether actively or otherwise, any plan or doctrine advocated by the 'prophets', seers, and revelators' of the Church is cultivating the spirit of apostasy. Lucifer...wins a great victory when he can get members of the Church to speak against their leaders and to 'do their own thinking.' When our leaders speak, the thinking has been done. When they propose a plan - it is God's plan. When they point the way, there is no other which is safe. When they give direction, it should mark the end of controversy."
>
> (*Improvement Era*, June, 1945, p. 354)

And yet, with no mention of prophets, Jesus said,

> *"I am the Way, the Truth and the Life. No man comes to the Father but by me."*   (John 14:6)

There was no way around it. The Bible and the teachings of the Mormon Church were diametrically opposed. Even though the Church claimed to revere the Bible, in actual practice they put it below the doctrines of the Church. Where the two conflict, the Bible is ignored by saying it is not translated correctly.

No longer did I see my choice as being one of accepting or rejecting President Kimball's edict. Now I saw my choice as lying between the authority of the Bible and the authority of LDS Church dogma.

This was not a question of submission on one point concerning the place of blacks in the Church. It was a question of authority. Who had real authority? Did the Church have the right to exercise control over the lives of individuals when Scripture directed each believer to have a personal relationship with Christ?

The Bible claims God as the source of all authority, yet the LDS Church exercised its absolute priesthood authority in every facet of the lives of Church members, and there has been no change in the intervening years.

For a year, I studied the Bible intensively at home and with church study groups. I was thrilled time and again to find God's Word easy to understand and meaning just what it said. The Mormon Church's position that the Bible is not trustworthy because of incorrect translations never materialized as reality. The more I studied the Bible, the more its truth stood out. This could not be reconciled with the Mormon teaching that if the Bible contradicted Mormon teaching, it was because it had been translated incorrectly or that a particular verse was not inspired (LDS Articles of Faith #8). God's Word could not be written off so easily.

If I were to continue my life as a devout Latter-Day Saint, I would have to ignore hundreds of Bible verses, which never seemed to appear in the prepared lessons sent out from Salt Lake City to the entire church body. Searching the Scriptures for myself, I found too many verses to dismiss lightly, and as I found these great truths, I felt that I was looking into the mind of God, Himself. Instead of feeling confined and restricted, I felt free. Instead of confusion in my thinking, I found simplicity and clarity of thought which brought peace to my heart. The fog of eighteen years in the Mormon Church lifted slowly but surely.

Their reasons for claiming that the Bible is full of contradictions and inaccuracies became clear! Anyone taking the trouble to read it for themselves would find multiple verses that contradict Mormon teaching! They weren't willing to run that risk.

My Bible began to clear up the confusion in my mind. I could see its clarity and cohesiveness, and verse after verse became meaningful to me. I underlined each one in red and soon my Bible was a mass of red underlining! I felt that I could trust what It said. After all, even Jesus quoted from It as His ultimate authority:

> *"It is written..." He said. "Man shall not live by bread alone,*
> *but by every word that proceeds from the mouth of God"*
> (Matt. 4:1-11).
>
> Isaiah 40:8 says, *"The grass withers, the flowers fade,*
> *but the word of our God stands forever."*
>
> Matthew 24:35 says, *"Heaven and earth will pass away,*
> *but My words shall not pass away."*

Not only was it impossible for me to deny the truth of these verses, I didn't even want to try!

CHAPTER FOUR

Faith Demands Action

It was exciting to uncover God's truth. That year of study passed quickly, and I was happy to find that Jesus had become my constant companion. Instead of a complicated set of rules and myriad activities to fill my days, I had a Friend who walked with me through every day and in every situation and eloquently spoke to me through His biblical word.

For a long time, I had been so busy trying to achieve perfection in the Latter-Day Saints' system that there had been little time to even think of Bible doctrine let alone to have any kind of fellowship with the Son of God. Now His Presence on a daily basis brought new peace which began deep inside, warming my cold, pressured, empty inner self.

Jesus was receiving me with great love and the words, "Him that comes to Me, I will not cast out." Mormon teaching, however, demanded good works for salvation in statements like these in *Mormon Doctrine* by Bruce R. McConkie:

> "Thus it is that men are not saved...by merely confessing the Lord Jesus with their lips but rather by doing the will (good works) of the Father which is in heaven" (*Mormon Doctrine*, pg. 329).

> "This doctrine of good works is that men, based on the atoning sacrifice of Christ, must work out their own salvation in the kingdom of God (the Mormon Church)" (*Mormon Doctrine*, pg. 330).

> "To gain salvation after baptism, it is necessary to keep the commandments of God and endure to the end" (*Mormon Doctrine*, pg. 118).

Still, the Bible says,

> "If you confess with your mouth, the Lord Jesus and believe in your heart that God has raised Him from the dead, you will be saved. For with the heart man believes unto righteousness, and with the mouth confession is made unto salvation" (Rom. 10:9).

Nor is there room for works in a truly Christian salvation:

> "By grace are you saved through faith, and that not of
> yourselves; it is the gift of God - **not of works**, lest
> any man should boast" (Eph. 2:8-9).

Despite my deep entrenchment in the legalism of the Mormon Church, the close relationship with Jesus that I had experienced as a teenager began to reassert itself. I felt sad as I read,

> I am amazed that you are so quickly deserting Him who called
> you by the grace of Christ, for a **different gospel**; which is really
> not another; only there are some who are disturbing you and
> want to distort the gospel of Christ. **But even though we, or an
> angel from heaven,** should preach to you a gospel contrary to
> that which we preached to you, let him be accursed. (Gal. 1:6-8).

It was as though the words had been written especially for me. I had known Christ and had left Him for "another gospel" which Joseph Smith claimed had been revealed to him by Moroni, "an angel from heaven."

The false doctrines of Mormonism are consistently inconsistent with biblical Christianity. Those "revelations," the contradictions within Mormon teachings that subvert biblical doctrines, caused me to decide to resign my membership in the LDS Church. Now I knew that my commitment was to Jesus Christ, *"the Way, the Truth and the Life,"* (John. 14:6), relying solely on His consistent, unchanging Word.

"...He saved us, not because of righteous things we had done, but because of His mercy" Titus 3:5 NIV.

Since then, I've learned that the solid conviction that comes from knowing God's Word always demands action on our part. We cannot just know it and go our own way. Knowing the truth and living the truth go hand in hand. The only way to ignore Bible truth, is to deny it. Then you can go on in your sin. But when it becomes clear and you accept the validity of it, your life will change. Someday, looking back, we will be able to say that we became like Jesus even though we could not see it at the time.

I didn't know just how unsettled all of my biblical discoveries had made my wife, but my decision to leave the Church had a decisive effect on her. She withdrew all affection, and I was isolated in my own home.

Her father, a Mormon High Priest, was not willing to put up with the "dictates of our own conscience" and pronounced dire warnings over my head! He assured me that there would be a loss of all spiritual blessings if I went through with my decision.

Suddenly, our marriage was incompatible and our home became a war zone. I had committed the ultimate sin of denying the "truth" of Mormon teachings. In less than a year, my wife divorced me. In another year, she was remarried to a "faithful Mormon elder." I was devastated!

For eighteen years, I had devotedly cared for my family and loved them unquestioningly. Our three children needed their father. The vows we had made in our temple marriage "for time and all eternity" were for a family that was to be "forever." At no time had I understood that our marriage was conditional on my acceptance of church policy. I thought I had entered into the marriage breathing, "*What God hath joined together, let no man put asunder*" (Mk. 10:9).

Once again, I turned to God's Word. This time, I was looking for comfort and relief from the anguish of my circumstances. I found these things and much more. What happened in my heart was not just healing, it was a miracle!

I was alone. No one had witnessed to me. No pastor ministered to me. No ministry to Mormons had provided me with materials and guidance against LDS doctrines.

I had only read God's Word and found its truth to be clear and undeniable! Jesus had been quietly living in my heart as I wandered the barren lanes of Mormonism, but He was there! He never left and when I sought Him, I found Him waiting patiently to open my eyes to His love and His truth. Now at this lowest point of my life, separated from home and family, He strengthened me and carried me through the valley.

He even gave me understanding and grace so that I was not overwhelmed by bitterness or vindictive thoughts. I did not set out to be hateful to those who sought to discredit and destroy me. I became a regular part of a Christian church fellowship and began to realize the joy of sharing in the family life of a church where Jesus is honored above all else. I began to relinquish command of my own destiny and allow God to accomplish His will in my life.

Nevertheless, I could not drop my many friends and family members in the Mormon Church just because they had turned their backs on this "wayward" man. I wrote to my local Church bishop that I chose "to follow Christ's direction in my life and not that of the prophet." I also said that I wished "to have my name removed from the Church of Joseph Smith, Spencer Kimball, or any other fictitious name it chooses to call itself."

What followed was unreal to the point of being unbelievable. I was summoned to a High Council Court which was to "consider the matter" of my resignation. What needed consideration? Article of Faith No. 11 said that I was free to follow God "according to the dictates of our own conscience."

Then why was I being put on trial? What "evidence" was going to be put forth?

I considered staying away and letting them hold their court and pronounce whatever sentence they chose. I wanted out, and obviously they were going to have the last word. Ex-communication would be my sentence. Since Mormons believe they are the "only true church," their determination to have absolute control was well known to me.

However, I decided to use the occasion as a time to give my testimony concerning Christ in my life. If He was at work in me, what did I have to fear? I invited several friends to come along as witnesses. However, the Stake President allowed no outsiders to come in with me.

This was in stark contrast to my baptism where I was urged to invite as many of my friends as possible. Now upon my departure from the Church, my friends were left waiting in the lobby while I was led to a large conference room and seated at one end of a twenty-foot table. Around the far end of the table sat the entire High Council.

Without any formal beginning, much less a prayer, one of the High Priests read the "evidence" - my letter of resignation. I was asked to acknowledge the letter and to comment on its validity. There was a sense of unreality about the entire proceeding. The men, some of my best church friends, were very somber and seemed to be completely incredulous that such a request had been presented.

It was a paradox: I felt as though I were the one sitting in judgment on them as they tried to explain the Church's attitude towards blacks based on the revelations of Joseph Smith and Brigham Young.

I responded with James' words,

> *"If you show partiality, you are committing sin..."* (James 2:9).
>
> "God is not one to show partiality, but in every nation the man who fears Him and does what is right is welcome to Him" (Acts 10:34-35), and
>
> *"Go, therefore, and make disciples of all nations..."* (Matt. 28:19).

Although it made no difference that day, it was just a little over a year later (from April 25, 1977 to June 8, 1978) that Prophet Spencer Kimball said he received a new revelation from God that the Mormon Church would now accept Blacks. Apparently God had changed His mind even though previously (according to 3 Nephi 2:14-16 in *The Book of Mormon*), Blacks who had become converted **had become white** as they were faithful to the truth and "their curse was taken from them."

This notice was published in the *L.A. Times* on January 13, 1979:

MORMON TELLS OF REVELATION ON BLACKS

SALT LAKE CITY (UPS) - Mormon Church President Spencer W. Kimball has revealed for the first time the conflict he experienced when he received the revelation from God that blacks should receive his church's priesthood.

Kimball said he sat in the Salt Lake temple with his Council of Twelve apostles in a prayer circle and "knew the time had come."

The church leader broke his silence on the revelation process in an interview in the church's Deseret News.

Kimball announced last June 8 that the Mormon priesthood would be open to "all worthy male members," including blacks, who had been excluded from full participation in the church for its 148-year history.

"I went to the temple alone. It went on for some time as I was searching for this, because I wanted to be sure. We held a meeting of the Council of the Twelve in the temple on the regular day. We considered this seriously, thoughtfully and prayerfully. We had this special prayer circle, then I knew that the time had come. I had a great deal to fight: of course, myself, largely because I had grown up with this thought that Negroes should not have the priesthood and I was prepared to go all the rest of my life till my death and fight for it and defend it as it was."

"But this revelation and assurance came to me so clearly that there was no question about it."

About a week after the trial, I received the following letter:

The Church of Jesus Christ of Latter-Day Saints
La Crescenta California Stake
La Crescenta, California 91214

May 3, 1978

Dear Brother Hall:

This letter is written to officially notify you of the action of the High Council Court that was convened the 25th day of April 1978 in the High Council Offices: You have been, by action of the court, excommunicated in conformity with your request. (*My request was to resign, not to be excommunicated.*)

The pronouncement of excommunication presented to you at that time means that there has been a complete severance from the church and that you are no longer a member and will be denied all the privileges of membership. Tithing and other contributions are not to be given to the church in your name; however, they may be held on deposit for a later time when they can be presented in your name or they can be made to the church in the name of your family members in good standing.

As is the case with all non-members, you will be welcomed to attend sacrament meetings, auxiliary meetings, and Public Conference Sessions.

You are denied the greatest blessings that your father in heaven
has to offer his children, that of membership in his church
and participation in its full program. It is our prayer that you
might consider this action to be only temporary in your life.
You're encouraged to let your life follow good directions
and to associate only with those persons who are of a high
character and who live good Christian lives with obvious
intentions only to do good to their fellow men. We encourage
you to pray continually for the Lord's blessings in your life.
It is our prayer that some day you will feel disposed to once
again come into the church through baptism and join in full
fellowship with those of us who have known and loved you.
Be assured that you have our love and deepest considerations
at this time.

Sincerely,
Your brethren of the Stake Presidency

I wanted to accept this love and concern expressed at face value, and I did act on it in that manner. However, in my heart, I knew that their "caring attitude" would not last long. I never counted on it even though I tried to maintain my Mormon friendships as long as I could.

Resigning my membership in the LDS Church was never an option. Resigning means only one thing to church leaders. By leaving the "only true church," you are automatically considered an apostate. A church-instigated temple divorce from my wife was the ultimate "denial of blessing" I was to suffer, however, I knew my decision to leave this organized hypocrisy was one I would never regret. Without a doubt, God's word initiated my decisions by revealing the biblical Jesus and biblical Christianity *in all its fullness*. In spite of all the heartache of the church prompting my wife to break up our family, the Lord has restored to me "the years that the swarming locust has eaten... Who has dealt wondrously with you; and my people shall never be put to shame" (Joel 2: 25,26).

CHAPTER FIVE

A New Passion

Eighteen years of my life had evaporated as though they had never been. I felt a compelling need to find a purpose for that expenditure of life and time. Also, I had learned a lot about biblical answers for false Mormon teachings. I had something to say to those who blindly followed these fallacies. If I could bring someone out of that darkness with me, the agony and loss would all make sense.

That fall (1978), I was introduced to members of the newly formed ministry, Ex-Mormons for Jesus (EMFJ). Others who had left the Church felt as I did. There was a need for ministry to those left desolate by the empty doctrines of Mormonism. A new conviction gripped my heart - love for Mormon people was demonstrated by former members zealously reaching out to them with God's truth. There was also a need for a support group for those who dared to step away from that Church and follow Christ without reservation!

I had tracts printed telling my personal story which I mailed to many Mormons I had known, especially those who had been very close to me. I had no idea what reaction I would get. I only knew that it was important to speak my convictions to those who were important to me.

Here is that first tract:

How Anti-Mormon Literature (the Bible)
Led Me Out of the "Third Ward"

(The Testimony of Tom Hall, an ex-Mormon for Jesus)

MORMONISM: "A PRAISE TO THE MAN"
(LDS Hymn No. 147)

Singing praises to Mormon prophets in LDS hymns such as "Praise to the Man," "Come, Listen to a Prophet's Voice," and "We Thank Thee, O God, for a Prophet" were just one indication to me that more time was spent relating to these "seers and revelators" than to Jesus Christ Himself. It also became obvious to me that my fellow missionary companions, known as "seventies," were disclaiming the reliability and translations of the Bible. The Word of God was, however, the main force that turned my life around. I committed myself to Jesus Christ alone, and I began trusting in Him to point the way in my life and not a so-called prophet of God, for the Bible verses in Hebrews 1:1-2 told me in no uncertain terms that "*God, who spoke in times past by the prophets; in these last days speaks to us by His Son.*"

God's gift of life is the time He gives us to fulfill His purposes in our lives. He wants us to be a witness to His plan for our lives and His true church: the body of Christian believers who follow Jesus as "the way, the truth, and the life." In order to fulfill this responsibility, I cannot ignore the years I spent trying to find Christ in the Mormon religion.

As a high school English teacher, several of my students had questioned me about my membership in the Mormon Church, and I dutifully referred them to our local missionaries. I could not, however, offer my Black students this invitation to investigate the church. I was a hypocrite no matter how I tried to rationalize the discrepancy in the LDS church policy of denying the priesthood to Blacks which, indeed, denied them the most important privileges of being a Mormon. I did not have to wait for President Kimball to have a new revelation concerning this problem, for God had already spoken to me through Bible passages such as the following:

> James 2:9 "If you show partiality, you are committing sin…"

> Galatians 3:28 "There is neither Jew nor Greek, there is neither bond nor free, there is neither male nor female: for ye are all one in Christ Jesus."

> Acts 10:35 "…God is not one to show partiality, but in every nation the man who fears Him and does what is right is welcome to Him."

When I began to really study the Bible, I realized the beauty and truth of Jesus Christ's way of life was in direct opposition to that of Mormon doctrine. Having Jesus take over my life and trusting completely in Him has meant more to me than any church system or Mormon "way of life." Men are fallible and subject to Satan's influence; I could not allow a feeling or "different" Christ or special person alter the truth that is evident in God's Word, the Holy Bible.

I am convinced that receiving Jesus as my personal Savior when I was in my teens provided the working of God's Holy Spirit to lead me out of the darkness of Mormon doctrines. In all those eighteen years of repetition and programming of the LDS church system, a persistent and nagging question was simply, "Where is Jesus and why is He so obviously overshadowed by the "living prophet" of the Mormon Church?"

As a Mormon, one is expected to sustain and submit to the priesthood authorities who are supposedly given the keys to direct members or "call" them to positions and jobs within the local church "ward" or "stake" boundaries. A member should never rely on a personal relationship with God to direct him in a particular calling; it is up to the ward bishop or stake president. They have the keys of authority to assign members to service positions for the upbuilding of God's Kingdom on the earth and also act as an indisputable guide for solving your personal problems.

The Bible promise in John 8:32 indicated to me a much different point of view: "If you abide in My Word, you shall know the truth and the truth shall make you free." I Corinthians 2:10,11 states, "For to us God revealed them through the Spirit...for who among men knows the thoughts of a man except the spirit of the man, which is in him?" I Cor. 2:16 "For who has known the mind of the Lord, that he should instruct Him? But we have the mind of Christ." Psalm 119:105 "Thy Word is a lamp to my feet and a light to my path." Ephesians 3:20 "Now to Him who is able to do exceeding abundantly beyond all that we ask or think, according to the power that works within us."

The freedom of Jesus alone to guide me and direct me through life is surely a perfect fulfillment of these verses. My life in the Mormon Church was dependent on the will of other men.

I saw it in the robot-like existence and blind obedience to a system that predominated so many church activities. Even testimony meetings provided little variety as most seemed an endless chain of repetitive monologues that had little to do with God's direction in one's life.

Young men and women are "called" by their bishop to serve as missionaries and they accept their new role as a duty to the church rather than a personal calling from God. Mormon doctrine seems to ignore the following Bible passages that give Jesus the ultimate control in one's life through the simple act of accepting and acknowledging Him.

> John 14:6 Jesus said, "I am the way and the truth and the life: no man cometh unto the Father but by me."

> I John 4:4 "Greater is He that is in you than he who is in the world."

> Acts 17:28 "For in Him we live and have our being."

> Romans 10:9,10 "...if you confess with your mouth Jesus as Lord, and believe in your heart that God raised Him from the dead, you shall be saved; for with the heart man believes, resulting in righteousness, and with the mouth he confesses, resulting in salvation."

MORMONISM: A GLORIFICATION OF SELF

Mormon doctrine states, "As God is, man may become; as man is, God once was." In other words, Mormons believe that God was once a sinful man in another world where He began His progressive perfection to become one of perhaps millions of gods having jurisdiction over their own created worlds. Sound far-fetched? Just ask a Mormon! Does it sound biblical? No wonder the Bible is rated low in accuracy from a Mormon point of view!

As I was engulfed in the LDS Church program, the idea of working toward godhood began to overshadow the relationship I had known with Christ as my personal Savior. At this point, I began to acknowledge myself as the only dominant force to accomplish salvation and I proceeded to "do it my way." My testimony was flawless; my feelings told me this was the way God's plan of salvation was meant to operate. After all,

"The glory of God is intelligence" and this Mormon motto became the sole criterion for working out my salvation.

I am so thankful that Jesus never abandoned me even though I turned my back on the promptings of the Holy Spirit to realize the blatant errors of Mormon doctrine as compared with the basic truths of the Bible. It was truly a revelation to read the Bible and see page after page of Scripture that was in total opposition to Mormon theology.

Proverbs 14:12 spoke loudly and clearly to me, *"There is a way which seems right to a man, but its end is the way of death."*

The Mormon way was filled with pride-producing titles and awards and an endless variety of pseudo-leadership positions (in name only) that give a person the feeling of importance and achievement. I had become a victim of my own self-esteem and began to "lean on my own understanding," which is exactly what the Bible tells us we should not do. Proverbs 3:5

"Mormonism uses the same terms that Christians use, but they are not the same in meaning. Therein lies the trap. The unwary person hears of the joys of the gospel, the love of Christ, and God's desires for us and then steps into the realm of the subtle 'doublethink': Christians falling prey to a missionary teaching plan not given out of the hearts of the young men there in your home, but created by some of the cleverest sales psychologists in the world." (Ed Decker, *To Moroni With Love*).

The basic Mormon missionary approach reveals very little that would appear to be in conflict with the Bible, and the basic doctrine of the church which would identify it as a cult is tactfully ignored until one has been sufficiently indoctrinated to accept it. If I had studied the Bible and realized the full significance of Christ's message there, I certainly would have found that the following Mormon doctrines were nothing but a perversion of biblical truth:

1. **All churches except the Church of Jesus Christ of Latter-Day Saints (Mormons) are in error; they are all abominations before God.** (Joseph Smith, *History* 1:14-19)

2. Mormons claim to be Christian, but reject biblical doctrines and have no association with Christian churches whatsoever. (*Mormon Doctrine*, p. 136)

3. Christ's death on the cross paid for Adam's transgression only, and we are saved only to be resurrected and then judged for our works. (*Mormon Doctrine*, p. 669)

4. We must each earn our own salvation to achieve the highest degree of heaven; there is no hell as described in the Bible. (*Mormon Doctrine*, p. 329)

5. The Bible is at best a weak source of truth. It is in error and its teachings about salvation are inadequate. (*Mormon Doctrine*, p. 82)

6. We can become gods. (*Teachings of Joseph Smith*, pp. 345-347)

7. God was once a sinful man but "progressed" into godhood as did our "heavenly mother." (One of God's polygamous wives, not to be confused with Mary.) (*Doctrine and Covenants*, pp. 19-32; *Mormon Doctrine*, p. 516)

8. Members of the church must accept the dictates of a living prophet, for he has direct communication with God and is an infallible source of direction for their lives. (*Mormon Doctrine*, p. 606)

9. Temple marriage and rituals are necessary as a means of achieving godhood and the highest degree of heaven. (*Mormon Doctrine*, p. 117)

10. Your ancestors can only be saved if temple work is performed on their behalf. (Proxy baptism and "endowment" ceremonies.) (*Mormon Doctrine*, p. 822, "Vicarious Ordinances")

By definition, a cult embraces one or more of the following tenets: They humanize God, deify man, minimize sin or ostracize the Scriptures. Mormonism uses all four to bring forth its false doctrines. It is not a Christian church. It is a cult that hides behind a facade of Christianity.

As the cults continue to entice great numbers of unwary people to their ranks, I feel obligated to reveal the deceptions that were responsible for my acceptance of Mormonism.

At the same time, it is my prayer that those who became my friends, "brothers and sisters" in the Mormon Church, will open their hearts to the Word of God and receive Jesus Christ alone for the direction in their lives.

In Christ,
Tom Hall

In my weakness and immaturity as a Christian, I had allowed Mormon doctrine to submerge my relationship to Christ. I had blindly followed their teaching that "As God is, man may become; as man is, God once was." I let them direct my life into fruitless striving to reach godhood.

I allowed what I knew of God to be lost in the maze of "eternal progression." He became just one of millions of gods who had earned their way into godhood. The Mormon motto at Brigham Young University, "The Glory of God is Intelligence," became the sole basis for working out my salvation and exaltation.

The appeal to my pride, the friendships that filled a void in my life, the similarity in terminology - all these combined to lure me into the Mormon sidetrack that dead-ended when I resigned from "The Church."

The titles and leadership positions conferred on new converts gave me feelings of importance and achievement. Their plan and approach worked perfectly for me. I felt important. I felt that I belonged. I felt I was achieving.

How meaningless those titles and positions became - how empty was my relationship with God when it was based on my feeble works of righteousness!

The fact that Mormons use the same terminology Christians use had given me a feeling of familiarity even as a new-comer. The thing I hadn't realized was that the terms meant something entirely different than what I had previously understood. 'The joys of the Gospel,' 'the love of Christ,' 'God's plan for us', etc. all sounded right. How was I to know that new definitions had been applied to each phrase?

Exalting faithful Church members would alarm those who read II Thessalonians 2:4 which speaks of Satan,

> "He exalts himself over God and even proclaims himself to be God."

This is the goal of works in the Mormon Church - to become gods! "As God is, man may become," is often repeated as the ultimate achievement for faithful LDS. Then, each one sets out to accomplish enough good works to achieve that lofty goal. But the Bible tells us that,

> *"We are all as unclean thing, and all our righteousnesses are as filthy rags"* (Isaiah. 64:6).

The impossibility of becoming gods is clearly stated in Isaiah 42:10,

> *"...before Me there was no God formed, and there will be none after Me."*

Still, the LDS Church claims to accept the Bible...or wherever it is "translated correctly" (LDS Article of Faith #8). Was this some kind of inaccurate translation? The next chapter of Isaiah (44:8) says again,

> *"...is there any God besides Me? I know of none."*

If God (Who knows everything) doesn't know of the millions of gods in the Church of the Latter-Day Saints, then who are these gods? They can only be imposters and the church system that produces them is a lie from beginning to end.

Proverbs 14:12 warns us,

> *"There is a way which seems right to a man, but its end is the way of death."*

This is a perfect and complete description of the Mormon Church. However, when a Mormon missionary comes to your door, he speaks of little that appears to conflict with the Bible. The basic doctrines of the LDS Church that would identify it as a cult are tactfully ignored... at first. Then when the convert is sufficiently indoctrinated and can tolerate their bizarre teachings, he will accept doctrinal positions without too much question.

By every criterion, Mormonism is a cult. They deify man, they humanize God, they deny the Word of God and they minimize sin as God defines it. Mormonism is not a Christian church! These are the things I wanted to say to my Mormon friends.

I mailed out at least thirty of my tracts. Although many in this group had been my very close friends, there was not one single response until a year later when I heard from the adult Mormon missionary, Ellis Craig, who had presented the LDS "plan of salvation" to me.

Here's what he said,

> Dear Friend Tom:
>
> I have been carrying your four page (I hardly know what to call it, it is so full of hurt and hate) typed tract mailed to me on May 23rd with me in my briefcase.
>
> Except for the brief note you penned at the top of your - MORMONISM: A "Praise to the Man" diatribe, I would not have believed that the kindly, reasonable friend and brother I know as Tom Hall could have possibly written it.
>
> Tom, I used the word "diatribe" because it means..."A discourse of bitter, malicious criticism and abuse." It is most difficult for me to connect that type of person with my Brother Tom Hall.
>
> I have waited all this time without answering because I suppose I hoped to receive another letter from you saying... "please forget what I have said in pain caused by the break-up of my family."
>
> I can only bear witness to you that Jesus is the Christ, that He is my Savior, that his true Church is THE CHURCH OF JESUS CHRIST OF Latter-Day Saints, that the only way we can enter the Father's Celestial Kingdom is through Jesus Christ and His True Church...by living the TRUE commandments of God, and remain true and faithful to the end.
>
> I know this and I know YOU knew it because I was with you when the Holy Ghost bore witness to both of us as we studied and prayed together in my office many years ago, and many times since.

The "Salvation" you now speak of is a GIFT from Jesus Christ
to EVERYONE...Resurrection and Just Judgement, regardless
of what one believes and EVERYONE is assured of a place in
either the Terrestrial or Telestial Kingdom of Heaven, (at
least). BUT the FATHER's Kingdom, called the Celestial
Kingdom, and the opportunity to become perfect..."Even as
My Father in Heaven is Perfect" is reserved for those who keep
the commandments of GOD through Jesus Christ and his one
and only true Church. Tom, I know you know this and I call
you back to reality, as your brother and in his Holy Name.

Faithfully,

Ellis

He denied my change of heart in spiritual things and laid my efforts to share the truth with him to hatred borne out of the painful loss of my family! I am glad that he recognized that I already knew all the trite phrases of the Church with which he filled his letter. He actually had not understood what I had said!

To tell the truth, I was shocked to hear from him at all, knowing how entrenched in Mormonism he was. I felt that I must have touched a raw nerve or he would not have responded at all. It got to me that he had put words in my mouth concerning my spiritual awareness and I didn't appreciate it. I felt obliged to answer as clearly as I knew how, and thus began a fourteen-month correspondence with Ellis based on God's Word.

Note: In the first printing of *Mormon Chronicles*, I used the name "George" as a pseudonym for Ellis Craig and paraphrased his letters in order to protect his privacy or cause him further animosity in our relationship.

While writing this new edition, *Mormon Chronicles of Deception*, I regretted to learn that Ellis had passed away. Sometime in the future, I had hoped our exchange of biblical vs. Mormon doctrines would make a difference in his trusting Jesus alone for eternal salvation.

The letters of dialogue between us in this book are now exactly as written, including punctuation, spelling, underlining, and grammar.

Dear Ellis:

It has been many years since we've had the opportunity to sit down and reflect on God's plan and purpose for our lives. Many times I have fondly remembered the love and concern you showed me by helping me realize the close bond that should exist in all relationships.

Ellis, you are a distinct and rare person with a great capacity to love your fellow man. Whether you realize it or not, the place you've had in my life has been one of monumental importance. Ultimately, it brought me to the full realization of who Jesus Christ is and how he can also be our personal friend as well as our Lord and Savior.

I'm not surprised with your reaction to my testimony for I realize that you have been hearing the Mormon "way of life" preached as the only true way since you were born.

It has taken a great amount of courage and conviction to step away from the "security blanket" the Mormon Church offered me, but God has the power to affect changes that are for our best interests in Him and eternity.

Your letter indicated that what I said in my tract was because of the break-up of my family. This is totally inaccurate. I began questioning the LDS doctrines against blacks in 1975, and it was from this spark of inconsistency with the Bible that I began to study the Bible in earnest.

No person and no church tried to influence me. I discovered so many contradictions from what the Bible said that to continue as a member of the LDS church would make me the most bigoted and hypocritical person I could imagine. God's Word has stood the test of time and fulfilled prophecy. I do not rely on a feeling to test the Book of Mormon, for the Bible has spoken to me directly.

The true church of Jesus Christ is alive today as it always has been through the priesthood believers in all Christian churches. Jesus said that the gates of hell would not prevail against His church and I fully accept this prophecy. He also said that where two or more are gathered in His name, He is there with them.

Ellis, I have visited many Christian churches and find the same prevailing fellowship in spirit and oneness in Christ alone. My wife admitted that she filed for our divorce with my leaving the church as the prime motivator. Even the bishop of our ward admonished me to leave my own home and seek a legal separation. In fact, his law firm handled the divorce!

Since my self-imposed "excommunication," you are the first Mormon to speak to me or offer the slightest amount of concern or love.

Ellis, I love you as a brother and all the church members I have ever known, but I must place my faith in God alone, not a church system. Since my acceptance of Jesus as Lord of my life in 1945, He has never left me. I was just too wrapped up in myself to realize what His way, truth and life really means. I was too complacent to study His Word, but I thank Him for finally leading me to discover what He has said. It's all there just waiting for us.

I was astonished, for instance, to read the Book of Romans and understand so clearly what the law of God means to a follower of Jesus Christ. Above all, I love my Lord Jesus, for He's alive and with me every living moment of my life. I hope we can see each other soon.

In His Love,
Tom

CHAPTER SIX

The Mormon Progression

At this point, I bring you those letters, which show the direction that Mormon friends take when you don't fall in line with Church doctrines. Note that Ellis's initial letter identified me as a friend, ("Dear Friend Tom"). Then in succeeding letters, he becomes formal with "Dear Mr. Hall," followed by a final salutation of "Dear Former Friend." He rejected me as his friend because I no longer held the same church teachings he holds. I was outside his realm and unworthy to have a part in his life any longer.

Nevertheless, I tried to explain how I discovered the truth written in the Bible and what it really says as well as my reasons for feeling compelled to accept its authority above all other writings. I expressed my thanks for his writing to me at all since that was the first contact I'd had with any of my Mormon friends since leaving the Church. With all the sincerity I had, I assured him of my love for my Mormon friends in spite of my trust in God alone rather than a church system. I confessed the years of my sinful pride and my willingness to go along with obviously false teaching rather than to search for the truth. Most of all, I told him of my gratitude to God for holding onto me in spite of my biblical ignorance.

Before I share these letters with you, it's crucial that we discuss the difference between the Mormon Jesus and the Jesus of the Bible. You will then realize that Mormons and Christians are not worshipping the same Jesus.

Mormons are instructed to say something like this: **"We believe in Jesus as you do. The name of Jesus Christ is in our church name, the Church of Jesus Christ of Latter-Day Saints. Of course we are Christians."**

However, this was not always true. In 1830 when the church began, the official name was "the Church of Christ." (*Doctrine and Covenants* 20:1) In 1834, there was a unanimous agreement by the members and leaders of the church to remove Christ from its name. The official church name became "The Church of the Latter Day Saints." (*History of the Church*, Vol. 2, pg. 63) The name of Jesus Christ did not re-appear until four years later. (*Doctrine & Covenants*, Section 115)

Here are just a few doctrinal statements that confirm the radical difference of the Mormon Jesus to the biblical Jesus:

"But under certain circumstances there are **some serious sins for which the cleansing** (blood) **of Christ does not operate,** and the law of God is that **men must then have their own blood shed** to atone for their sins." *(Mormon Doctrine*, p. 92)

Read **I John 1:17** ALL SINS are cleansed and forgiven by Christ's blood.

"There is no salvation outside the Church of Jesus Christ of Latter-Day Saints." *(Mormon Doctrine*, p. 670)

Read **Acts 16:31** Salvation based firmly on Jesus and faith in Him.

"If it had not been for Joseph Smith and the restoration, **there would be no salvation**." *(Mormon Doctrine*, p. 670)

"...no man or woman in this dispensation will ever enter the celestial kingdom of God **without the consent of Joseph Smith**..." (Brigham Young *Journal of Discourses*, Vol. 7, p. 289)

Read **I Timothy 2:5** Christ is the only mediator between God and Man.

"The appointment of Jesus to be Savior of the world was contested by one of the other (spirit) sons of God. He was called Lucifer...**this spirit-brother of Jesus** desperately tried to become the Savior of mankind." (Milton Hunter, *The Gospel Through the Ages*, p. 15)

Read **John 1:1-3** Jesus is God!

"Christ was begotten by an Immortal Father **in the same way that men are begotten** by mortal fathers." *(Mormon Doctrine*, 1979 edition, p. 547)

Read **Matthew 1:18-20** Conceived by the Holy Spirit.

"...**Jesus Christ was married at Cana of Galilee,** that Mary, Martha and others were his wives, and that he begat children." (Brigham Young, *Journal of Discourses*, Vol. 2, p. 210)

Read **Genesis 2:24** God's standard of having one wife.

> "…for we know that it is by grace that we are saved, **after all we can do**."
> (II Nephi 25:23)

Read **Ephesians 2:8,9** Salvation is the gift of God, not of works.

> "We believe that through the Atonement of Christ, all mankind may be saved, by **obedience to the laws and ordinances of the Gospel**."
> (3rd Article of Faith of the Mormon Church)

Read **Ephesians 2:8,9** Salvation a gift of God, not of works.

> "**I have more to boast of than ever any man had**. I am the only man that has ever been able to keep a whole church together since the days of Adam. A large majority of the whole have stood by me. Neither Paul, John, Peter, nor Jesus ever did such a work as I. **The followers of Jesus ran away from Him; but the Latter-Day Saints never ran away from me yet**…"

> (Joseph Smith Jr., *History of the Church*, Vol. 6, pp. 408, 409)

The preceding statements by the doctrines and quotations of the very highest Mormon Church authorities were discovered by me only after I began to follow the apostle Paul's advice to, "**Prove all things**." Even Jesus quoted scripture when being tempted by Satan! (See Matthew 4)

Ellis didn't answer my December, 1980 letter so I sent him the following tract in January, 1981.

What Is a Cult?

Beware of another "gospel": Gal. 1:6-9, II Cor. 11:3-15, II Tim. 3:1-16 and 4:3-4, Col. 2:8-23, Prov. 14:12.

The Marks of a Cult
How You Can Know One When You See One

1. **Deify man:** Say that man may become God; man needs only to progress (with the cult's help) to become like God. Gen. 3:1-13, Isa. 14:9-19 (the very same sin of Satan), II Thes. 2:3-4.

2. **Humanize** God: Deny that God is one eternally. Deny the Trinity. There are many gods, and redefine God to man's image. Rom. 1:21-25, Isa. 43:10-11 and 44:6-8, Ps. 90:2.

3. **Minimize Sin**: Instead of man's very nature being separate from God, sin is only specific acts that through good works can be perfected. Hell is redefined. Rom. 3:23, I Jn. 1:8-10, Gal. 3:10, Rev. 20:14-15.

4. **Ostracize the Scripture**: They will add additional scripture and claim that there is error in God's Word. Continual change of scripture. Lk. 21:33, Rev. 22:18-19, Isa. 40:8, Acts 17:11.

5. **A Different Jesus**: Jesus is not God the Son, but rather a son of God; a prophet; a created God; our elder brother. Isa. 9:6-7, Jn. 1:1-14, Col. 1:15-20 and 2:9-10, Heb. 1:1-12.

6. **A Different Salvation**: Deny salvation by grace, by the shed blood of Jesus on the cross (usually see no cross on their churches). Must have works plus a system dictated by the cult. Eph. 2:8-10, Gal. 3:1-26, I Peter 2:24.

7. **A Different Spirit**: The Holy Spirit is changed into a "force" or impersonal entity. Not God the Spirit. Spiritism is generally rampant and visits from familiar spirits, counterfeit miracles, etc. I Tim. 4:1, Deut. 18:9-14, Jn. 14:17.

8. **A Modern Day "Prophet"**: Founded by a man, followed by others, who claim to be God's one true spokesman on earth. Give revelation and scripture. Jer. 23, Matt. 24:24, Heb. 1:1-2, Deut. 13:1-10, 18:20-22.

9. **The "Only True Church"**: Their group is the only way to perfection. The word "truth" used over and over. Unless you follow their organization, you are lost. Deny the spiritual union of believers. Col. 1:18, Eph. 1:22-23, Rom. 12:1-8.

10. **Secrets**: Closed to Outside: Secret rituals, temples, doctrines. Finances not public. No communion with others in Christian body. All others are outsiders. No one knows certain "truths" as they (and their prophets) do. Persecution complex.

11. **Cannot Leave:** Always testing your loyalty. Obedience is primary. Leaders have power and are your intermediary, not Jesus. Only way to leave is by excommunication, threats. Cut you off. Spiritual bondage. Fear. Guilt.

That got a response! Ellis correctly pointed out that we couldn't both be right! In his mind, he believed that I was accusing him of "living evil principles, taught by evil men." However, he asked me which church I would recommend; he was still looking at institutions, not seeking a personal Savior.

Dear Tom:

I have your short OFFICE MEMORANDUM note before me, with the SUBJECT noted as I Thess. 5:21 "Prove all things; hold fast that which is good." I also have your "THE MARKS OF A CULT" which deals with some of the things you are AGAINST...but it is difficult to know what you are FOR.

You speak in your note about "the love Jesus has for us in His uncluttered Gospel," yet the things you now talk about are a disjointed mass of clutter.

What is the REALITY you wish to expose me to? Years ago I taught you the reality of the LIVING CHRIST whom I love and worship in the manner HE has commanded. I love and worship HIS FATHER IN HEAVEN who is MY FATHER IN HEAVEN. I seek the companionship of THE HOLY GHOST by living the Gospel of JESUS CHRIST to the best of my limited ability. I fully understand the meaning of the "Oneness" enjoyed by these three glorious, perfect, separate BEINGS.

I know the REALITY of the fact that unless YOU and I are ONE in CHRIST, we are not HIS! Considering your present attitudes, it is impossible that we both could be correct.

I honestly treasure the early years of your membership in the Church. I know we were close Brothers in Christ. ONE in Faith, Baptism, Dedication to true principles, Brotherhood and Love of Christ. I know that ONENESS was REAL and CHRIST-LIKE. I KNOW the HOLY GHOST bore witness to both of our Souls that the CHURCH OF JESUS CHRIST OF Latter-Day Saints was the true church of Christ and will remain so until the Millennium when Jesus will return in Glory to assume personal leadership of it on Earth.

I know you are a good man and that the Grace of Jesus Christ will therefore save you in the Terrestrial Kingdom of Heaven, unless you continue to hate and fight his True Church. But I want you to be saved in Our Father's Kingdom, the Celestial Kingdom, and I want to be there with you, with all our friends and loved ones who love the kind, generous, loving and faithful Latter-Day Saint you used to be! NOT the vindictive, hate spouting, apostate sounding ANTI-person you seem to be now. I cannot believe that you, think I am an evil person, living evil principles taught by evil men. I AM very CONCERNED about you and I want to be your true friend and brother.

What CHURCH would you have me join? Does it have Apostles and Prophets? Or don't you believe the Lord when He says they are necessary? Who would you have baptize me? By what authority? Would he have received Priesthood Authority as Aaron received it? Would he believe we could become perfect… "even as our Father in Heaven is perfect?" Through faithfulness to Christ? Come back home, Tom.

Love, Ellis

It dawned on me that Ellis had done what most LDS missionaries do; he ignored the points in the "What Is a Cult?" tract and wrote about other things entirely! His accusations of hatred and vengeance sounded familiar too. It was another stock response Mormons use when faced with truth they cannot refute.

I decided to focus on Jesus as the only way to God as long as Ellis remained open to discuss faith and truth with me. I urged him to read the Bible for himself. His letter revealed that the simplicity of the gospel of Jesus Christ had escaped him. "Believe in the Lord Jesus Christ and you will be saved" was too straightforward and simple to be grasped by a person steeped in layers of requirements and dogmas, the levels of achievement and works of righteousness found in Mormonism. He was still hung up on churches and their "systems,"missing Jesus, the One who is the Truth.

He saw the Mormon Church as a "way of life" and could not shed the "Oaths and Covenants" which had been so ingrained in his thinking.

He referred to "the very **center CORE** of a faithful Latter-Day Saint's life," but I was unsure of whether he harkened back to Jesus or to the temple and "the sacred covenants" made there. Somehow I doubted that he considered Jesus to be the center core of his life. Clearly, the temple was the heartbeat of life for "worthy" Mormons everywhere. Temple work had to be carried out in the place and in the manner prescribed by the Church to qualify for salvation in the "Celestial Kingdom" of God.

Ellis's letter revealed the standard Mormon misperception, the belief that Christian churches have nothing in common doctrinally and have no fellowship with each other. Because Mormons are isolated, they perceive every other denomination to be isolated when in fact, the large majority of Christian churches hold to the great common body of truth found in the Bible. Most of them recognize God's Word as the ultimate authority and claim Jesus as Savior of the world, **the only Mediator between God and man**(I Timothy 2:5).

I wrote my next response to Ellis's invitation to "come back home" to the "priesthood authority" of the Church of the Latter-Day Saints.

Dear Ellis:

I assume you are living in Salt Lake City on a permanent basis now, but please call me when you're down this way. I'm really shocked with your openness to at least remain friends with me. Most LDS, in fact **all**, have totally rejected my desire to maintain an occasional visit with them. All I can surmise is that I pose some sort of threat to their sanctity.

I certainly do not hate the Mormon people, but have a commitment with Christ not to be ashamed of His gospel and share its joy with whomever I may encounter. I also do not feel that you or any other LDS is **purposefully** accepting an evil doctrine or belief. On the contrary, my motivation is only the intense love God has given me to all mankind (including the Blacks) and I'm sure my handicapped children helped me see and accept the precious and distinct gift of life we all share.

Your concern for me deals with a church system of men and **their** "authority."

I cannot accept something that is so completely in contradiction to God's Holy Word. When Christ was crucified, the veil of the temple was rent! "In the past, God spoke to our forefathers through the prophets, but in these last days He has spoken to us by His Son…" (Heb. 1:1).

Only Jesus has the authority. He is the only High Priest in our lives (Heb. 9:11). Christians are a "royal priesthood" with only Jesus as our shepherd. We have His assurance that **only He** is "the Way, the Truth and the Life" (John 14:6).

In Revelation 3:20, "Here I am! I stand at the door and knock. If **anyone** hears my voice and **opens** the door, I will go in."

That obviously means we have a **personal** Savior who will come to any man who asks Him. His life and crucifixion mean nothing if we accept the works-for-salvation principle of the Old Testament (and LDS).

Only Jesus is **worthy,** for our works are as "filthy rags" (Isaiah 64:6). When He enters your life by your undivided commitment to Him, He accomplishes the works, not **you.** He makes the perfection possible, not you.

This, dear brother, is the reality I wish to expose you to, and only He and He **alone** has the power to do it.

Jesus declared Himself to be God and was crucified for it. He said, "I and the Father are One." If this is wrong, His position as Savior is of no consequence, for we would still be judged for our **works** to attain salvation.

By acceptance of Christ in my life, I do the works because I love Him and I **want** to. There are no guilt trips for me anymore; my salvation in His kingdom is assured, and He did it for me as the Lamb of God, and now I have Jesus as my constant companion and He speaks to all who accept Him as the Lord of their lives. "In times past, God spoke through the prophets." He speaks today to you and me **personally** if we but **receive Him** and the gift He offers us, eternal life! He receives all the glory and praise. God bless you as you read His Word, dear friend, **especially** the Book of Romans.

Love in Christ,
Tom

I now understand why isolation from the Christian body of believers is necessary to keep Mormons from seeing the false prophecies and claims made by Joseph Smith and Brigham Young, et al. If Mormon leaders were to honestly compare what they believe (for instance, the requirement of having a living prophet as God's spokesman) with the Bible, they wouldn't hold to it. As long as members are isolated - diverted from studying the **entire** Bible one-on-one with **contemporary** translations - it's easy to be kept in ignorance of the overwhelming power of its truth.

As a Mormon, I was taught to accept **only** the King James Version of the Bible as the finest translation available, and no wonder! With so many archaic words no longer used in present-day English, it was very easy to miss God's message entirely!

Two verses in Hebrews are an example of this. Every Mormon should know and understand them, yet the King James language covers up the meaning:

> "God, who at sundry times and in diverse manners spoke in
> time past unto the fathers by the prophets, hath in these last
> days spoken unto us by His Son, whom He hath appointed heir
> of all things, by whom also He made the worlds" (Heb. 1:1-2).

Compared with today's English usage:

> "In the past, God spoke to our forefathers through the
> prophets... but in these last days (He) has spoken to us
> by His Son" (Heb. 1:1-2).

Both versions are equally correct translations which unequivocally state that Jesus is the fulfillment of the prophets, and God speaks directly to us "by His Son," but how easy it is to miss that point in the 1600's King James Version with all the thees and thous, begats and begots, etc.

A month passed before receiving a new letter response to a phone call I made to Ellis, trying to convey the difference God's Word was making in my life.

> Dear Brother Tom:
> Thank you for the telephone call last Sunday, I appreciated it,
> but I can't honestly say I fully enjoyed it. I do not enjoy not
> being united with you in our faith and believing.

I will be pleased to meet with you any time we can both make it. I love you as a brother and I wish to continue my friendship with you.

I am really surprised that you don't realize that I know the Doctrines of the Baptist Church...backward and forward, and that you evidently believe that your discussions of them with me would be persuasive new information to me. Except their mode of baptism, their doctrines are a mass of confusion, in my opinion. Their simplistic "Believe on Jesus Christ and you are saved" approach is most effective, especially with those that do not view Christianity as a complete way of life.

Have you blocked your mind and your conscience regarding the Oath and Covenants you made in the most HOLY place of Christian worship...with the LORD JESUS CHRIST? Where you learned the TRUE order of Worship of the LORD...and the part PETER, JAMES AND JOHN and ADAM occupy in that TRUE FORM of worship? Of course you know that I am talking of the TEMPLE and the sacred Covenants you made there with the LORD JESUS CHRIST... the very center CORE of a faithful Latter-Day Saint's LIFE.

The LORD JESUS CHRIST requires that we worship HIM in "HIS OWN WAY!" and "HIS OWN WAY" is taught to the faithful in HIS HOLY HOUSE...the TEMPLE!

Is it necessary for me to remind you Tom...that God will not be MOCKED? You have been in the HOLY TEMPLE and you KNOW whom the Latter-Day Saints worship... the LORD JESUS CHRIST, in the way our FATHER IN HEAVEN taught HIM.

You also now seem surprised that the Lord taught those that also MOCKED him in JOHN 10 verse 34... "Jesus answered them...Is it not written in your law, I SAID ye are gods. Verse 35: If he called them Gods, unto whom the word of God came, and the Scriptures cannot be broken."

Of course the LORD was reminding them of PSALM 82, Verses 6 and 7..."I have said, Ye are gods; and all of you are children of the Most High. If HE called them gods, unto whom the word of God came, and the scripture cannot be broken."

Tom, I look forward to seeing you...but I will not argue with you.

Luv, Ellis

A favorite Bible Verse (John 10:34) commonly used by Mormon missionaries has to do with a statement made by Jesus which refers back to Psalm 82:6,7. At face value, they take it to mean that Jesus taught that men could be gods. In the context of the Old Testament situation, it becomes clear that God was speaking of judges in the land of Israel. He was telling them to judge justly, defend the poor and to deliver the poor out of the hand of the wicked. He said, "*Ye are gods; and all of you are children of the Most High.*"

First of all, notice that the "g" in gods is a small letter. The original language clearly does not refer to deity but to leaders among men - **judges**. Their authority and responsibility set them up as agents of God, the Most High, and it was His justice they were to deliver.

Next, we must go on and finish the statement quoted in the Psalm. Verse 7 says, "*But ye shall die like men, and fall like one of the princes.*" God does not die but the judges are told that they will indeed die and fall just as princes (another kind of leader empowered by God's authority) die and fall.

The Psalmist goes on to implore God that He be the One to judge the earth; "for thou shalt inherit all nations."

The statement goes like this: "Ye are gods...but ye shall die like men." No matter how high a position a man may hold in his lifetime, death is the end of his power on earth.

How like the LDS Church to take one small phrase out of its context and build out of it an entire doctrine which controls the lives of its members, pushing them relentlessly to reach higher, toward the goal of godhood.

Instead, we have a huge body of truth that runs from Genesis to Revelation that tells us that God alone is God and there is no other. It is inconsistent and unreasonable to say that these many verses are translated incorrectly while this one small phrase is the basis for an entire Church dogma.

I thought that if I could present enough biblical references to the importance of a Christ-centered life, Ellis would be able to realize that Jesus did it all. There are no works needed. He alone is worthy. My next letter, along with the main Scriptures that attest to God's grace apart from good works, was mailed in hope of making the point valid.

Dear Ellis:

I agree with your last letter in that it is important for us to be united in our faith with Jesus as the "very center core" of our lives. The hate you say I now have for the Mormons can only be a defense mechanism that implies persecution. Nothing could be further from my mind; **I am only defending the Word of God and its inalterable message**, the message that has set me free from LDS doctrines and the manipulation of men. It is the re-awakening of Jesus Christ as the Lord of my life and a personal Savior who dwells in me, not just a figurehead at the top of a priesthood hierarchy.

My only wish is that you will put aside the rules and regulations of Mormon theology and immerse yourself in the Bible. It has all the direction with Jesus at the helm of my life. **This** is what I lean on, not the Baptist Church or **any** church system.

I think you will agree that men working with their own understanding can deviate from His Word very easily without realizing what is happening; the many religions and cults testify to that fact.

I remember a statement you once made, "If the Mormon Church were not true, Joseph Smith would have committed the greatest hoax ever perpetrated upon mankind." This would have some accuracy if Jesus had not been the fulfillment of all the prophets (Heb. 1:1) and the law. **Joseph Smith was never a part of God's plan according to this Scripture.** (See Matt. 5:16 also)

Ellis, I have a great burden for the Mormon people. I was there for eighteen years. I know the bondage that can overwhelm a person caught up in all the busy work it encompasses. The Bible says our "works are as filthy rags in His sight" (Isaiah 64:6).

The law ended because as we have an inability to keep it; we must invite Jesus to come into our lives. At that time, He takes over and begins to fulfill a work in you that is according to His Lordship over you, not yours or any other man's. He alone makes it possible for our lives to change, not the futile attempts we make, but the in-dwelling Spirit He provides! I praise God for this gift He offers all mankind.

I've indicated on the enclosed sheets some of those Scriptures that attest to the validity of His merciful grace. The comments after each scripture just relate to the subject matter. Ellis, I pray you will at least read those areas **in context** and offer Jesus a reply. This is the evidence that demands a verdict and a commitment. I can never thank Him enough for what He does in my life and the joy it brings in **His** righteousness, not my own!

Tom

CHAPTER SEVEN

Free at Last

M y letter to Ellis reiterated my dependence on the Bible - not people or churches, but God's Word. Also, it seemed important to me to let him know how free I felt after eighteen years of busy work which amounted to nothing but "filthy rags!" (Isaiah 64:6).

I also sent him a list of 53 Scriptures which (if he would read and compare them with Mormon doctrines on those various subjects) would show him God's truth. (Look for this list in the back of the book.)

It is not possible that Ellis could have considered the Bible verses on my list since in his next letter, he claimed to "believe each and every one of them." If he really believed them, he could no longer have been considered a good Mormon because every single one is contradictory to Mormon teaching.

Again, Ellis retreated inside the Church restating the LDS familiar claim that the Bible can only be translated within the framework and boundaries of the "only True Church." He closed with a promise of his undying loyalty to me and a declaration of my worth.

In response to my efforts to convey my personal relationship to Christ and His Word, he wrote:

> Dear Tom:
>
> Thank you for your letter. I appreciated the several pages of Scripture quotations. However, since you know that I believe each and every one of them, your hard work was wasted motion.
>
> Of course I know our chance for salvation and Eternal Life (God's Life) would be nil without the glorious GRACE of JESUS CHRIST!
>
> It is OBVIOUS that we, all of us, are now as 'filthy rags' WHEN COMPARED WITH JESUS CHRIST and OUR FATHER IN HEAVEN! Even my children who get up every week day morning at 6:15 A.M. to have family Scripture reading...know THAT!

They also know, and so do you, that the Lord said many times…"If you Love Me, keep my commandments!" They know, and so do you, that learning what HIS commandments are…and KEEPING them, is what GOOD WORKS is all about. BECAUSE of the Grace of Christ which has SAVED every one of us from physical death and has assured every one of us of a righteous judgment…we have THE FREE AGENCY to choose which Kingdom of Heaven we will live in FOREVER…("In My Father's house there are MANY mansions," etc.)…by the way we KEEP the Commandments.

Tom, I know, and so do you, that the Glorious Gospel of Jesus Christ as taught by HIS True and Authorized Church, is a COMPLETE way of life which acts as a Schoolmaster to lead us to the Perfection of our God, our Father in Heaven who has placed CHRIST as our Head. Of COURSE we are ALL imperfect…but He has given us the principle of REPENTANCE by which we can day-by-day rid ourselves of our weakness and receive each day the healing GRACE OF JESUS CHRIST and receive of HIS STRENGTH so that we may grow worthy to have the daily companionship of The HOLY GHOST… John 14:26. "But the Comforter, which is the Holy Ghost, whom the Father will send in my name, He shall teach you all things, and bring all things to your remembrance, whatsoever I have said unto you."

Tom, I know that YOU know the interdependence of GRACE, FAITH and WORKS. The fact that we are NOTHING without the GRACE OF CHRIST does not cancel out the Lord's COMMANDMENTS! I know that YOU KNOW because I taught you. Your hang-up regarding WORKS is beneath you… it is just one of the results of your Apostasy which is a very unhappy, thorny path to travel.

One Quotation SHOULD be enough…James 2:14-20 "What doth it profit, my brethren, though a man say he hath faith, and have not works? Can faith save him? 15. If a brother or sister be naked, and destitute of daily food. 16. And one of you say unto them, depart in peace, be ye warmed and filled; notwithstanding ye give them not those things which are needful to the body; what doth it profit? 17. Even so faith, if it hath not works, is dead, being alone. 18. Yes, a man may say,

Thou hast Faith, and I have works; show me thy faith without they works, and I will show thee my faith by my works. 19. Thou believest that there is one God; thou doest well; the devils also believe, and tremble. 20. But wilt THOU KNOW, O VAIN MAN, THAT FAITH WITHOUT WORKS IS DEAD?"

You say in your letter of March 18, that you "have a great burden for the Mormon people." BURDEN? At the same time you laugh and say how happy you are! You are wounded and hurt!...but happy??

The NAME of the TRUE CHURCH is THE CHURCH OF JESUS CHRIST OF Latter-Day Saints. It is HIS Church. I KNOW that Joseph Smith is a True Prophet of God and that he was CALLED, ORDAINED and TAUGHT under the direction of JESUS CHRIST and the AUTHORIZED PROPHETS HE sent. I KNOW that JESUS CHRIST has kept his promise made to his original Apostles...THAT HE WOULD RESTORE HIS CHURCH IN ITS FULLNESS IN THE "LAST DAYS" BEFORE HIS SECOND COMING. THE AUTHORIZED WORK OF THE MINISTRY IS NOW BEING CARRIED OUT UNDER THE DIRECTION OF JESUS CHRIST HIMSELF...THROUGH HIS APOSTLES AND PROPHETS...WORLD WIDE! THE MOUTHPIECE OF JESUS CHRIST FOR HIS CHURCH...TO THE ENTIRE WORLD...IS PRESIDENT SPENCER W. KIMBALL.

I know these things to be true and the day will never dawn when I will not remind you of those facts...and bear witness of Jesus Christ and His True Church...you will never lose me because you are my Beloved Brother and you are too important to me and your Brothers and Sisters and to your FATHER IN HEAVEN, the Father of us ALL.

Love,
Ellis

His argument was some kind of spiritual doubletalk. His long explanation of James 2:14-20 shows that he missed the point of that passage completely! Far from saying that we must do good works to be worthy of salvation, James says that the natural outgrowth of faith is good works as surely as the planted seed sprouts the plant of its own kind. The fruit of faith is good works!

Others can't see your faith, but they can see your good works, and these good works should tell them that you have faith. To carry this line forward, to conclude that we are saved by these good works contradicts the clear teaching of many other Scriptures.

From the entire teaching of the Bible, it is impossible to conclude that we are saved by our works. So, coming to such a conclusion means to bypass and ignore many other passages such as,

> For by grace are ye saved, through faith, and that not of
> yourselves, it is the gift of God, not of works lest any man
> should boast (Eph. 2:8-9).

Salvation is by the grace of God - a gift! Salvation "is not of works lest any man should boast!" I heard a lot of boasting in the Mormon Church. Again, consider the boast of Joseph Smith:

> "*I have more to boast of than ever any man had.* I am the only
> man that has ever been able to keep a whole church together
> since the days of Adam. A large majority of the whole have
> stood by me. Neither Paul, John, Peter, nor Jesus ever did it. I
> boast that no man ever did such a work as I. The followers of
> Jesus ran away from Him; but the Latter-Day Saints never ran
> away from me yet" (*History of the Church*, Vol. 6, p. 40).

Ephesians 2:10 goes on to say that since God has saved us, He has also "foreordained" that we should accomplish many good works during our lifetimes. This is not some small distinction! It is a basic, fundamental difference in doctrine which leads believers in opposite directions. Those who believe they can achieve salvation by good works grow proud and self-righteous. Those who depend on God for salvation, offer their lives in service to others (that's "good works") out of hearts of gratitude for what God has done. What may appear similar on the outside, is vastly different on the inside!

My response to this letter was a re-statement of my faith and fellowship with Jesus Christ in my renewed life. I hoped to show him that I needed no one between myself and Jesus to interpret God's message.

Dear Ellis:

The enclosed is probably the closest parallel (Jeremiah 18:6) I can find to exemplify my life in Jesus. "He is the potter, I am the clay." You say that I only keep proclaiming my love for Jesus, but that does not build His Kingdom, and you're in agreement with Matthew 7:21, "Not everyone that saith unto me, Lord, Lord..." and I also am in agreement. But Ellis, that Kingdom will only be built with Christ, alone, not in human regulations that are subject to Satan's influence and the prideful nature of men, but by **LIVING IN HIM**.

The Bible warns us against such deceit, Colossians 2: 6,7,8,9,10.

(6) "So then, just as you **received** Christ Jesus as Lord continue to live **in Him**,

(7) Rooted and built up **in Him**, strengthened in the faith as you were taught and overflowing with thankfulness.

(8) **See to it that <u>no one</u> takes you captive through hollow and deceptive philosophy, which depends on <u>human tradition</u> and the basic principles of this world rather than on Christ.**

(9) For in Christ all the fullness of the Deity lives in bodily form, Father, Son, Holy Spirit,

(10) And you have this fullness in Christ, who is the head over every power and authority."

When you lean on His Word and His authority, Ellis, you cannot falter in the ways of this world.

As I continue to study His Word, the inalterable message is the same. He speaks to me on a daily basis that eliminates any middle-man.

When Spencer Kimball received a "revelation" on the status Blacks should be given in the LDS church, he must have been unaware that the Bible **already** makes it plain. "God is **not** a respecter of persons," "all men are the same in His sight," "go ye into **all** nations..."

This is not an "intellectual cave" I withdraw into, Ellis. Rather, "It is for freedom that Christ has set us free" (Gal. 5:1). "I have been crucified with Christ and I no longer live, but Christ lives **in me**."

When Christ returns, His church will be ready. Nothing that we alone can do will make it so.

Love in Christ,
Tom

That he understood! His next letter said, "You say over and over... 'I love you, Lord Jesus!' " (Yes, indeed, that's what I said!)

Dear Tom:

Thank you for your letter. Your letters are a puzzle in that they would indicate that they were written by someone who does not know the doctrines, ordinances, priesthood system and function of The Church of Jesus Christ of Latter-Day Saints.

But of course you and I know that you DO know them...or should know them. The fact that you have turned your back on them and the Holy Covenants you made with Jesus Christ in His Holy Temple...does not make them GO AWAY!

No one in THE Church has given, or is giving you a hard time. Your Free Agency and Freedom of Choice is respected by your Brothers and Sisters in the Church. But that does not block out the concern and affection that I and many others in the Church have for you.

I know that YOU know that all your concern that THE Church is a Cult is just plain foolishness. Something that is an exact Restored by Authority DUPLICATE of the ORIGINAL... is that exact opposite of a Cult! *It is unnecessary for me to comment on the 11 Points in your WHAT IS A CULT? printed sheet.* You know the truth as well as I do. You have for the time being turned your back on it. *I have faith that the Tom Hall that I knew and respected will face the cause of his unhappiness and confusion which resulted in your "Flip Out"...and will take the proper correction steps.*

It is not my intention to make light of any of the things I have discussed above. It is difficult to choose words that express what I honestly feel and think without sounding undiplomatic.

I DO care about what you think and feel. But what you say to
me in your letter seems to me to have so little SUBSTANCE.
You say over and over...I LOVE YOU LORD JESUS!! But
you are not willing to KEEP HIS COMMANDMENTS or
serve in HIS Church which is DIRECTED BY HIM through
HIS APOSTLES AND PROPHETS. That is too HUMAN.
But are not ALL of us HUMANS, GOD'S CHILDREN?

Faithfully,

Ellis

Ellis **rightly concludes** that anyone who loves Jesus will keep His
commandments, but he added - "and serve in His Church which is
directed by Him through His apostles and prophets." Deftly, he moved
all the LDS Church doctrines between himself and Jesus Christ while
I was telling him that Jesus and His Word are all he needs.

His accusations against me were that I had turned my back on
my temple vows, I had "flipped out," and that I was a hypocrite
unwilling to keep God's commandments. Sadly, I suppose what he
said was true...from his perspective. **If** the temple vows and the
Church's interpretation of God's commandments were true, then **I
surely had deserted them both!** Ellis wanted to use my new-found
walk with Christ to say I had lost my faith.

The thing I hoped to convey to Ellis was that temple vows really are
a hoax. Also, it is unnecessary to let the Church interpret God's Word
for us; we can understand it for ourselves. Beyond all that, loving Jesus
gives us the inward desire to obey God's commandments. No one needs
to create "a complete way of life" in order to bring about conformity
to God's laws. He asked us to keep His commandments if we love
Him, so keeping His commandments is high on our priority list.

As a Mormon, I always felt guilty because I was trying to appear
to be holy, when deep down, I knew that I was far from it. I felt as
though Matthew had been written about me in particular,

"You are like whitewashed tombs, which on the outside appear
beautiful, but inside are full of dead men's bones and all
uncleanness" (Matt. 23:27).

There was no joy in obeying the rules and regulations of "the Church." Just the opposite! The more I tried to keep them, the more I knew I couldn't. The guilt that followed was a heavier burden than the dead weight of the Church commandments.

My disappointment was overwhelming that Ellis would not carefully consider the points concerning cults in the tract that I sent. So I turned to his comments concerning my wedding day.

I'd taken a blood oath that I found inwardly repulsive. I'd gone through the "endowment" ceremony like a robot. No teaching, no warning, nor any explanation had been given ahead of time.

Did they believe that I knew what to expect? Or were they sure that I'd do what I did, go through the motions and try to forget it. I was only gullible for eighteen years. Praise God, it wasn't a lifetime!

My compassion for Ellis made my next letter sound somewhat desperate. My attitude toward the church came through loud and clear. I only hope that my love and concern for Ellis came through to him as clearly.

> Dear Ellis:
>
> I had expectantly anticipated your response to the inconsis-
> tencies between Mormon doctrines and biblical Christianity,
> especially the eleven points that outline a cult. These points are
> crucial, for they are backed up with God's Holy Word in many
> scriptural references. If the Scriptures are not true, why? Which
> ones? Where in the Bible are these points incorrectly translated?
>
> I remember going to the LDS temple in L.A. without any idea
> what would take place that day and no one would tell me. I
> was forced* on my wedding day to take a blood oath in that
> temple when the Bible specifically warns against taking such
> oaths (James 5:12, Matt. 5:34-35). I remember the caricature
> of a minister portrayed as a tool of Satan, and the doctrine
> of the Mormon Church that all Christian churches are an
> abomination in God's sight. That means vile in God's sight!
>
> I know the LDS Church has a persecution complex and uses
> the idea that all satanic forces are at the bottom of this, but
> when one church steps apart from biblical Christianity and
> the body of believers with their demise as its main purpose,
> this is not the Church of Jesus Christ!

It is fruitless to put your faith in the hands of mortals. I implore you as a Christian to forsake the blasphemy of those evil doctrines that chain men to a system of works. Believe what the Lord has said in the Book of Romans about this. Read it over and over and over. The point is very clear. Your works of righteousness can only be wrought in Jesus' hands - not your own. Accept Him humbly as the Lord of your life for only He is worthy.

Certainly, the "pedestal" of the Mormon Church doctrines is no more than a "Tower of Babel," and the Lord will not be mocked by the assertion that you can achieve a place of godhood in the eternities.

I'll continue to pray for His will to be done in both our lives. You are indeed my very special friend and always will be! Jesus loves you and so do I!

Tom

*(Since my temple marriage required that I accept those blood oaths as part of the day's activity, without prior knowledge, I hardly could have changed my mind at that point. That is why I used the word "forced.")

If Ellis read and understood the love I sent him in that letter, he rejected it in his next greeting. From "Dear Brother Tom," we had taken a nose-dive to "Dear Mr. Hall!" His attack on me was ferocious.

Dear Mr. Hall:

Since I received your hypocritical letter, I have carefully reread our exchange of letters during the past year. I now fully realize that the kind, spiritual, faithful Latter-Day Saint who loved the true Gospel of The Lord Jesus Christ who was dedicated to the BUILDING of the Kingdom of God on Earth, who was honest and truthful, who LOVED the Lord and His TRUE CHURCH...THE CHURCH OF JESUS CHRIST OF Latter-Day Saints...who became my beloved Brother in CHRIST...TOM HALL, is now spiritually dead!

In his place has risen an un-Christian hatemonger, TOM HALL, spouting venom in the image of that pathetic fellow hatemonger, Walter Martin[2]. A TOM HALL who now mocks the Lord's Prophets and Apostles. A TOM HALL who spouts egregious lies about the Sacred Covenants he made with The Lord Jesus Christ in the Lord's Holy House...the Temple. A deliberate deceiver TOM HALL who whimpers that in ignorance he was FORCED to take oaths the first time he went to the Temple! When you continued time after time to go to the Temple to receive the great blessings to the Faithful... of your own FREE WILL, were you still ignorant? Were you still forced time after time? You LIE and the truth is not in you when you even hint at such a thing.

I, as the person who first taught you the truth of the restored Gospel of Jesus Christ...and who knows that the Holy Ghost bore witness to you of that truth, by the right of that knowledge and the authority of the Holy Priesthood which I bear, I call you to repentance. I seriously advise you to stop fighting the Kingdom of God on Earth. I plead with you to return to your rightful place in that Kingdom by humbly requesting re-baptism and membership in The Church of Jesus Christ of Latter-Day Saints.

In common sense, I ask you to look at the more than 700 Churches who teach conflicting doctrines, ordinances and practices in the name of Jesus Christ. Do you think the Lord is pleased with all these conflicts and contradictions? OF COURSE NOT! He has done exactly what he and his Prophets said he would do in the last days. HE HAS REESTABLISHED HIS TRUE CHURCH and the puny hand which you and other apostates hold up to stop it from filling the world will have no more effect than the futile but nasty spirit of the devil which you now serve.

Sincerely,
Ellis

---

[2]Walter Martin, Ph.D., author of Christian books related to cult systems.

He had re-read our entire exchange of letters and concluded that I had become an enemy of the "True Church" and had set out to wreak as much damage on it as possible. He called me a liar, a deceiver, a whimperer...a hatemonger. As my first teacher in "the restored gospel of Jesus Christ," he called on me to repent. He said I was serving the devil!

As I read Ellis's letter, my spirits rose and my heart began to rejoice that I had been set free of such mind control and oppression. How I praised God that day for setting me free from the yoke of Mormon bondage that tries to control our thoughts and actions by the "letter of the law." How I could relate to Jesus' promise, "You shall know the truth and the truth shall make you free indeed" (John 8:32,36). Paul said, "The letter [of the law] kills, but the Spirit gives life" (II Cor. 3:6).

In all his declarations about the Church, Ellis never spoke of having a relationship with Jesus Christ or even being in direct contact with him. No, Ellis spoke of prophets and seers of the Church, their authority over the Church and its members. He harkened back to the Mormon teaching that Christ's church disintegrated after His death until Joseph Smith was given the revelation to restore the church Jesus had failed to preserve. (*Mormon Doctrine*, pp. 42-46)

We need only to consult our history books to find that the church was never dead; it has flourished throughout the centuries. Jesus cannot fail. He accomplishes everything He sets out to do. He Himself said, "It is finished" as He hung on the Cross. Far from being defeated, Jesus finished the work His Father had sent Him to do.

"The gates of hell shall not prevail against it," Matthew wrote of the church (Matt. 16:18).

How could I get Ellis to open his eyes to God's truth? Only a week later, I wrote to him again.

CHAPTER EIGHT

Losing a Friend

It was with a feeling of already accomplished defeat that I wrote again to Ellis. His accusations had stung me, but his use of "Dear Mr. Hall" told me that his mind and heart were closed, not only to me but also to the truth. In spite of his rhetoric, his eyes were blind to anything beyond the teachings of the Church of Latter-Day Saints. He was as bound as if he wore chains, hands and feet.

With a sense of rising desperation, I wrote to tell him that my statements had not been based on my feelings but on the facts of God's Word. The LDS Church had always stated that every man has "free agency" to believe in God as he sees fit, yet he was cutting me off because I no longer saw things as he saw them. Couldn't he allow me that liberty?

> Dear Ellis:
>
> Again, you choose to believe what you want to believe, not what I have experienced in fact.
>
> Your letter also states I went to the LDS temple many times. That is just not true. The few times I attended after my wedding, it continued to be void of any spiritual awakening in my life. It was, in fact, very lacking in worship or praise to God as far as I could perceive. The robot-like, mechanical utterances of temple workers were far from spiritual communication that is from the heart.
>
> You say that I now serve Satan, but it is the Mormon doctrine that puts man first - wanting to be the center - wanting to be a supreme being. That was the sin of Satan, and that was the sin he taught the human race!
>
> Your last letter now refers to me as "Mr. Hall." Your rejections of my free agency to believe what the Bible tells me is true is certainly not brotherhood or love in any way, shape or form. It is typical of what most "indoctrinated" Mormons, my "brothers and sisters," have demonstrated to me and my "free agency."

I welcome your friendship, if it truly exists, and even if it doesn't, I still love you and pray that you just open your mind and heart and accept the only way, truth, and life in Jesus alone.

In Christ,
Tom

There was no answer from Ellis, so I wrote again about a month later. I was unwilling to let him go if there was any way to keep up our dialogue. How frightfully deep is the gulf that separates those who accept God's Word as their authority and those who do not. In talking with Mormons, it is even more difficult because they claim acceptance of the Bible as their authority when, in fact, they subvert it whenever it suits their purposes.

His reply only deepened my sadness for him, for now he seemed to comprehend what I was claiming as my experience and understanding of the gospel yet without finding agreement or accepting the truth of what I had said.

Dear Mr. Hall:
I am writing to reaffirm my testimony to you and to explain precisely why I must refer to you as "Mr. Hall."

It is apparent that you are no longer the fine Christian man I once knew. Your attacks on the True Church of our Lord Jesus Christ and His Prophets and Apostles are extremely objectionable to me.

You are without excuse. Do you not recall the times when the Holy Ghost verified the truth of the Restored Gospel to you and me?

In your last letter you said:

- Even the Baptist Church is unnecessary to your "Christian life."

- The Lord alone speaks to you every day.

- Joseph Smith was never a prophet according to Hebrews 1:1-2.

If this is true, why would the Lord go to so much trouble to organize His Church with Apostles and Prophets to have the authority over it..."til we all come to the unity of the faith..."

(Ephesians 4:11-13)? Is there unity today among the Christian churches? I'll repeat what I said to you before:

1. The name of the only true church is THE CHURCH OF JESUS CHRIST OF LATTERDAY SAINTS.

2. I KNOW Joseph Smith is a true prophet of God.

3. I KNOW He has authorized PROPHETS AND APOSTLES TO RESTORE HIS CHURCH IN ITS FULLNESS in the days before His second coming.

4. I KNOW THE MOUTHPIECE OF JESUS CHRIST TO ALL MEN IS SPENCER W. KIMBALL.

5. Our authority does not come from BOOKS. It is bestowed from the Lord through His Prophets and Apostles.

6. I KNOW all these things to be true and IF YOU REPENT you will again be my cherished brother.

I must now end our relationship since you're now displaying the attitudes of a typical apostate. Your un-Christian behavior is full of hate, and you no longer have any regard for the truth.

I know these things are true and I will always be ready to reaffirm my testimony to you.

The Church of Jesus Christ prohibits its members from downing other churches; however, it is the Lord's business about what HE SAYS TO HIS PROPHETS.

As long as you continue to fight against the TRUE CHURCH OF JESUS CHRIST, I cannot believe you love Him as you keep telling me you do.

When you come to your senses and repent, I will be there to welcome you back into FULL FELLOWSHIP, and to rebaptize you as a member of the CHURCH OF JESUS CHRIST OF Latter-Day Saints.

Sincerely,
Ellis

Again, without addressing the problems of Mormon teaching, Ellis aligned himself with their doctrine of prophets and apostles. Many times I have seen the organizational charts for "the Church" with the current Mormon prophet at the top, side by side with a picture of Jesus Christ! There is not one single shred of biblical teaching to support such positioning. Instead, Scripture says:

> "**At the name of Jesus**, every knee shall bow both in heaven and in earth." (Philippians 2:10)

In spite of his protest that the Church is never to put down another church, Joseph Smith said from the beginning that **all Christian denominations "are an abomination in God's sight"** (Joseph Smith, *History* 1:14-19). Christian clergymen were portrayed as Lucifer's hirelings in LDS temple rituals.

On the other hand, Mormons accept "new revelations" by their appointed prophets. They must continually add to and change their doctrines and their Scriptures whenever public scrutiny makes their position "too hot to handle" (e.g., polygamy, denial of blacks, temple rituals, etc.). Ellis, and other Mormons, are dependent solely on "feelings" as to the truth of Church doctrines. Mormon missionaries challenge their potential converts to test the truth of the Book of Mormon by praying that the Holy Ghost will cause a "burning in the bosom" when they read it. Thus the most important truths of life are discerned by feelings which are totally subjective.

John tells us to test the spirits (I John 4:1) since Satan is the great deceiver and can appear as an "angel of light." The test is to compare what we hear with what the men who walked with Jesus taught us - the true gospel of Jesus Christ.

- His gospel has never changed, nor will it ever change.
- He has known the truth since the beginning.
- He does not change and His word does not change.

(Hebrews 13:8)

Jesus taught us to love one another, even our enemies. Where was the love that Ellis had proclaimed for me? On the basis of not believing as he believed, he rejected me and withdrew his "friendship" along with every Mormon friend and acquaintance I had ever known!

"If we love each other, God lives in us and His love is made complete in us" (I John 4:12).

I could not withdraw my love and friendship from Ellis. I wrote to him again.

> Dear Ellis:
>
> I am confused by your reactions to my stand against the doctrines of Mormonism. You say I am led by evil forces and not by the truth found in the LDS Church system. I am saddened by your judgmental remarks against me as a means of justifying the "Mr. Hall" attitude you now assume, especially when all my letters have only dealt with very obvious and basic principles that are spelled out conclusively in the Bible. You are not attacking me. You are in conflict with the Bible, for everything I've written is referred to in a Bible Scripture to verify the significance of it. These are not just feelings such as your "I know" testimonies. Ask yourself, "How do I know?" Is it just a "burning in the bosom" feeling? Is it based on "newly revealed" truth that conflicts with the Bible?
>
> Why do you ignore the letters I have written? **You failed to answer even one of these scriptural references!**
>
> My experience as a Mormon was that our works of righteousness make us feel that we are good - above all, that we are better than others. Is that now what you are doing in this instance?
>
> The real test of being in the presence of God is that you forget about your works of righteousness altogether, for if we are in His hands, only He has the power to change us; certainly not by our "puny efforts" are we making ourselves "worthy."
>
> Yours in Christ,
> Tom

Two weeks later, Ellis replied.

> Dear Former Friend Tom:
>
> I am deeply saddened to bring to a close the brotherly relationship we enjoyed for many years.

In reply to your last letter, I can only reiterate the truth of my convictions. I no longer have any respect for the hatemonger, Tom Hall. That kind, loving Latter-Day Saint I once knew by that name...is DEAD!

The gentle-hearted, considerate church member I once revered remains a fond memory. That is why I will try to help free you from the evil forces which would destroy God's Kingdom on earth, The Church of Jesus Christ of Latter-Day Saints.

Come back home, Tom. Return to the only authorized Church of Jesus Christ. Use your many special abilities to teach your present associates who hate the truth. Teach them the truth they must know through membership in His only, true Church. Then they may realize what it takes to become worthy recipients of the Celestial Kingdom.

Faithfully,
Ellis E. Craig

He had cut me off this time! Yet, in his loyalty, he continued to offer me restoration if I would return to the Mormon Church.

Return to bondage? I could not bear the thought. Return to domination by self-seekers and deceivers? I would never willingly place my life in their hands again. I was fascinated that Ellis continued to write to me. I was engulfed by regret that he could not see the truth of God's Word and accept it for himself.

By the New Year, I was taking part in programs sponsored by Ex-Mormons for Jesus and speaking in churches about my experiences in the Mormon Church. I decided to send Ellis a tape of one of our seminars because it gave a good comparison of the teachings of Mormonism against the truth of the Bible.

His reply came soon. Now, he seemed to feel the desperation of knowing that it was highly unlikely that I would return to the Mormon Church. He must have sensed my intention of continuing to warn people against Mormonism. The essence of my warning is, as it was then, against being ensnared in the LDS system of works for the purpose of reaching godhood.

He lashed out and offered me the promise of gaining "the Celestial Kingdom!" How pale that goal seemed compared to daily fellowship with Christ and my eternal home with Him! No desire for godhood filled my heart. Instead, gratitude for God's forgiveness (in spite of my unworthiness) thrilled my soul and gave me the peace of a settled salvation - no longer in question or doubt.

On reflection, I could see that by walking in fellowship with Christ, I was becoming the kind of person I had been striving to make myself become as a Mormon. Only I couldn't do it for myself! Christ had to accomplish the miraculous change of making a self-centered, proud man into one who knows his unworthiness and the matchless beauty of His Savior! How comforting to me are the words of John.

> *"The law was given through Moses; grace and truth were realized through Jesus Christ"* (John 1:17) .

"Grace and Truth!" How they have transformed my life! And I found them through Jesus Christ alone. No wonder I love Him so much! He gave me life in Him.

> *"He who has the Son has life; he who does not have the Son of God does not have life"* (I John 5:12).

Once more I had to write to Ellis, but my letter is really to anyone caught in the web of deceit of the Mormon Church.

My heartfelt prayer and desire for salvation for any and all who suffer this bondage remains with me to this day.

> Dear Ellis:
>
> One year of letter writing and reasoning together has indeed revealed how divided we are. Despite your repudiation of me and biblical Christianity, I will continue to pray that you and all Mormons will give God's Word in the Holy Bible preeminence as God's authority in your lives.
>
> You continue to stress your relationship with "The Church," priesthoods, and general authorities of The Church of Jesus Christ of Latter-Day Saints (Mormons). Never once have you expressed what it means to know Jesus in a personal, indwelling relationship that He has promised to those who answer His call (Rev. 3:20).
>
> It has been aptly stated that the true church of Jesus Christ is not an organization but an organism! The body of Christian believers is tied together, Spirit bearing witness to Spirit through one authority, the Bible: "The grass withers, the flower fades,

but the word of our God stands FOREVER" (Isa. 40:8). I am not tied to any one Christian denomination. I fellowship in a local mainstream, evangelical church only as a matter of worship preference, but I'm free to attend any Christian denomination if they honor Jesus alone as "the Way, the Truth, and the Life" (John 14:6) and hold the Bible to be the inerrant and final Word of God! "So, we who are many, are one body in Christ and individually members one of another" (Rom. 12:5).

Imagine someone asking about the name of your church, Ellis, and you proudly answer, "The Church of Jesus Christ of Latter-Day Saints." This person might then say, "I believe in Jesus Christ and trust in Him alone, but I don't believe in Joseph Smith. Can I still join your Church?" Every Mormon knows this would be impossible since Mormonism teaches that the church Jesus established was lost, and it took Joseph Smith to restore it along with adding hundreds of nonbiblical doctrines.

However, Jesus said:

> "I will build My church and the gates of hell shall not overpower it." Matt. 16:18

Jesus is calling, Ellis, He stands at the door waiting for you to answer His knock (Rev. 3:20):

> "I am the door; if anyone enters through Me, he shall be saved and shall go in and out and find pasture." John 10:9

What wonderful promises He has given us of salvation and His constant companionship if we just submit our lives to Him, not to a church organization that teaches that you can become a god.

> "Our fellowship is with the Father and with His Son, Jesus Christ." I John 1:3

> "God is faithful through whom you were called into fellowship with His Son, Jesus Christ our Lord." I Cor. 1:9

> "I am in the Father, and you in Me, and I in you." John 14:20

> "He who has the Son has life; he who does not have the Son of God does not have life." I John 5:12

> "...so that Christ may dwell in your hearts
> through faith."   Eph. 3:17
>
> "...according to the power that works within us,
> to Him be the glory."   Eph. 3:20
>
> **"To Him be the glory,"** Ellis!
>
> The Mormon hymn, "Come to Zion, Come to Zion,"
> always sounded familiar to me. Isn't it ironic to discover
> that it's the melody taken from an old Christian
> hymn, "What a Friend We Have in Jesus!"
>
> In His Way, Truth and Life,
> Tom

Ellis never answered this letter, but the Bible gives us assurance that His Word shall "accomplish" and "succeed" in the purpose of which it was sent. It (His Word) shall not return to me empty. Isaiah 55:11.

Compare the separation of Mormonism from the truth of biblical Christian doctrines. The following scriptural references demonstrate the vast difference.

BIBLICAL COMPARISONS

Jesus is <u>the</u> Way through the biblical word of God

"...and you know the way to the place I am going."

"I am the way, the truth, and the life; no one comes to the Father but through me."   John 14:4, 6

BY GOD'S GRACE

"By grace you have been saved through faith, not of yourselves; it is the gift of God, not of works...for we are His workmanship, created in Christ Jesus for good works..."   Ephesians 2:8-10

"...they asked him, '**What must we do to do the works God requires?**' Jesus answered, '**The work of God is to believe in the one He has sent.**' "   John 6:29

"In the past, God spoke to our forefathers through the prophets; but in these last days He has spoken to us by his Son..."   Hebrews 1:1-2

"That if you confess with your mouth, 'Jesus is Lord,' and believe in your heart that God raised him from the dead, you will be saved."   Romans 10:9

"For God so loved the world that He gave his one and only Son, that whoever believes in him shall not perish but have eternal life."   John 3:16

"...for it is God who works in you to will and to act according to his good purpose."   Philippians 2:13

"There is one God and one mediator between God and men... Christ Jesus."   I Timothy 2:5

"Salvation is found in no one else, for there is no other name under heaven given to men by which we must be saved."   Acts 4:12

BY JOSEPH SMITH

Joseph Smith as a "Prophet"...through the *Doctrine and Covenants, Book of Mormon, Pearl of Great Price, the KJV Bible* "as far as it is translated correctly" (LDS 8th Article of Faith), plus Joseph Smith's Translation of the Bible (never used!) plus LDS Temple "Endowments" and "Vows" plus a vast system of "Melchizedek" and "Aaronic" Priesthoods plus their authority over all church members plus each and every current "prophet" president since Joseph Smith, Jr., founder of the Mormon LDS Church.

BY THE WORKS OF MAN

"To earn one's 'worthiness' in order to participate in secret Masoniclike temple ordinances leading to exaltation as 'gods' and 'goddesses.' ...in the same position that God our Father stands to us."   *Mormon Doctrine*, p. 784

"Mormons are justified by grace only after they have succeeded in achieving 'worthiness.' ...for we know that it is by grace that we are saved, after all we can do."   *Book of Mormon*, 2 Nephi 25:23

"We believe that through the atonement of Christ, all mankind may be saved, by obedience to the laws and ordinances of this gospel."

3rd LDS Article of Faith

Temple workers are sometimes referred to as "Saviors on Mt. Zion." Baptisms by proxy for the dead is a major temple work. "The(LDS) Saints are...redeeming their (un-baptized) dead from the grasp of Satan."   Morgan, *Plan of Salvation*, pg. 8

"Celestial marriage is the gate to an (earned) exaltation in the highest heaven within the celestial world."   *Mormon Doctrine*, pg. 118

The "Mormon gospel" is no different from "another gospel" warned against by the apostle Paul in Gal. 1:6-10. "Now, am I trying to win the favor of men, or of God? Do I seek to be a man-pleaser? If I were still seeking popularity with men, I should not be a bondservant of Christ the Messiah." The four gospels: Matthew, Mark, Luke, and John all state how Jesus alone provided the free gift of salvation!

MORE BIBLICAL COMPARISONS

	MATTHEW	LDS
5:17	Christ is the fulfillment of the law.	Require a living prophet.
6:19	Don't store treasures on earth.	Require two year's food supply.
6:25	Don't worry about food or drink.	Require two year's food supply.
6:33	Seek His righteousness, not ours.	Our works earn salvation/ exaltation.
7:1	Do not judge others.	"Court" trials/Priesthood authority.
7:15	False prophets come in sheep's clothing.	Using Christian terminology with different meanings.
7:16	Fruit of the Spirit; good works are natual outcome.	Works required for Mormon "Celestial Kingdom" heaven. Grace is insufficient.
15:9	Beware of rules made by man.	New "scripture:" *Book of Mormon, Doctrine & Covenants, Pearl of Great Price.*
16:18	"I will build my church, and the gates of hell will not stand against it."	Christian Church was lost; Joseph Smith restored the only "true church."
18:20	"Where two or three gather, there am I in the midst."	LDS Church has the only priesthood authority to act in God's name. All other Christian churches "an abomination" to God.
19:5	One husband/one wife - "two become one."	History and belief in polygamy; God has many goddess wives.
22:28-30	No marriage at resurrection.	"Eternal marriage" required for spiritual progression.
23:5	Pharisee's deeds were glorified to be seen by man.	Required good works to achieve "worthiness" and temple "recommend."

	MATTHEW	LDS
23:28	Appear righteous, but are full of hypocrisy.	Must live by myriad lists of rules and regulations to achieve "worthiness."
24:24	False prophets performing great signs.	Displaying "perfectionistic" attitudes and "great signs."

	ROMANS	LDS
3:10	No one is righteous.	Possibility of becoming perfect in this life.
3:12	No one does good.	We can progress to become gods!
3:20	No one keeps the law. The law tells us we are sinners.	Worthiness earned by becoming perfect.
3:24	Christians justified by His grace.	Justified by works of the law.
5:19	Sin came through Adam -righteousness through Christ.	Justified by works of the law.
5:20-21	Sins exposed by the law.	Justified by works of the law .
6:14	Under grace, not law.	Justified by works of the law.
7:23-25	Only Christ can rescue us from sin.	We have the capacity to be sinless. We earn our salvation/ exaltation.
8:1-3	No condemnation for those in Christ.	Good works are mandatory.
8:5	Live in the Spirit.	Rely on keeping the law.
8:11	His spirit in us.	Self-determination.
8:15	No fear in Christ.	Guilt-ridden, always in fear of failure.
8:28	In Christ, all things work together for good.	Self-effort, intelligence is God's glory.
10:4	Christ is the end of the law for believers.	Always working to achieve worthiness.
10:9-10	The heart believes, the mouth confesses for salvation.	No guarantees for God's eternal security.

	ROMANS	LDS
12:14	Bless your persecutors - don't curse them.	Condemnation and cursing to all detractors.
12:19	Don't take revenge.	Slandering those who voluntarily leave.
13:10	Love fulfills law.	Guilt, shame, and fear to measure-up.

	JOHN	LDS
1:1	Jesus ("the Word") is God.	Jesus not a triune God but a created son.
3:3	New birth needed.	There is no "born-again" provision to exemplify a new spiritual birth.
3:16	Believe and receive everlasting life by the grace of God.	Plus "all you can do" to achieve worthiness.
3:36	Reject Jesus as Lord and be judged.	Seek exaltation through priesthood.
4:24	God is spirit.	God was once a man who achieved godhood.
6:28-29	The work required is to believe.	Self-achievement to earn worthiness.
6:35	Jesus is "Bread of Life."	Church rules/regulations to become acceptable.
6:46	No one has seen the Father.	Joseph Smith claims he saw God as a glorified man.
8:31	Believe and know the truth.	*Book of Mormon, Doctrine & Covenants, Pearl of Great Price* + the Bible.
8:58	Jesus said, "I am."	Jesus is created being, not considered God.
10:7-9	Jesus said, "I am the door."	Jesus' life insufficient as savior. Works required.
10:33	Jesus is God incarnate.	Jesus is not God the Son, but a son of God.

	JOHN	LDS
10:38	Jesus and Father are one.	Jesus is the first-born son of God, Lucifer's spirit brother.
12:46	Christ is our light in the world.	The LDS prophet is God's mouthpiece to "the Church" worldwide.
14:6	Christ is the Way, Truth, and Life.	The LDS Church and prophet have all divine authority as the **only** way.
14:9-10	Jesus and the Father are one.	Jesus and the Father are separate beings with bodies of flesh and bone. Jesus is not God.
15:4	Christ dwells in fellowship with us (see also 1 Cor. 10:16).	No LDS teaching supports this doctrine.
17:11	Father and Son are one.	Jesus is not God, the son. He's a son of God (1st born). Lucifer is His spirit brother.
17:21	God is triune; Father, Son, Holy Spirit.	LDS doctrine denies monotheism (one God). Mormons believe they can become gods!

	ACTS	LDS
1:7-8	God's power from Holy spirit to those who receive Jesus as Lord.	Holy Spirit conferred only by the Mormon Priesthood.
4:12	Salvation by grace through Christ.	Salvation/exaltation by worthiness of member's good works.
5:29	Obey God, not men.	Strict obedience to LDS prophet and priesthood.
10:28	Call no man unclean.	Blacks are considered a cursed race, were denied full church membership until 1978.
10:34	God accepts all men.	LDS Priesthood denied to Blacks for 178 years.
13:38	Keeping the law doesn't justify men.	"Worthiness" received by keeping the law.

	ACTS	LDS
16:31	Believe and be saved.	Achieving perfection earns the highest salvation.
17:24	God not served by human hands.	LDS Temple work offers salvation for the dead.
17:28	We have life in Christ by accepting Him.	There is no true salvation outside the LDS Church.

	GALATIANS	LDS
1:6-11	Warns against "angels" from heaven coming with **other** gospels.	The (LDS) Angel Moroni directed Joseph Smith to find the Book of Mormon.
2:4-5	Warns against teachers of false doctrine.	False doctrines and prophecy taught by Joseph Smith.
2:16	We are only justified by faith in Christ.	Legalism of strict perfection to be justified.
3:5, 6	Belief only counts for righteousness.	Belief plus good works. Faith alone rejected.
5:22	Fruit of the Spirit is love, joy, peace.	Maintaining worthiness by accomplishments.

	EPHESIANS	LDS
1:7	Redemption and forgiveness by His grace.	Redemption by good works.
2:8-10	Saved by grace, a gift of God - not of works, should any man boast.	Both works **and** boasting.

CHAPTER NINE

"...and the Word was God" John 1:1

God is faithful to His Word and His promises offering us the strength, patience, and joy of living a Christ-centered life. Scripture is the sustenance that enabled me to realize victory over obstacles of spiritual deception and catastrophic illness. The daily challenges of life itself are no match for the victory of applying God's instruction to the perplexity of living.

> **"Thy word is a lamp to my feet and a light to my path."**
> Psalm 119:105

Jesus was my healing stronghold through the Holy Spirit for me to survive both lung and prostate cancers. Relying on just the Bible, God's Word also exposed Mormonism for all its deceitful practices. His Word has been such a precious discovery to influence the healing processes I needed to overcome Mormonism's and cancer's entanglements.

Jesus said,

> "I am the light of the world. **Whoever follows me** will never walk in darkness, but will have the light of life."   John 8:12

> **Commit your way to the Lord**; trust in Him and He will do this."   Psalm 37:5

> "**Trust in the Lord with all thine heart** and lean not unto thine own understanding. **In all thy ways acknowledge Him,** and He shall direct your paths."   Prov. 3:5,6

> "**The Lord is my shepherd** I shall not want. **He makes me lie down** in green pastures, **He leads me** beside quiet waters, **He restores** my soul. **He guides me** in paths of righteousness for his name's sake. Even though I walk through the valley of the shadow of death, I will fear no evil, **for you are with me; your rod and your staff,** they comfort me. **You prepare a table before me** in the presence of my enemies. **You anoint my head with oil; my cup overflows.** Surely (your) **goodness and love will follow me** all the days of my life, and **I will dwell** in the house of the Lord forever."   Psalm 23

What a blessing to meditate on these precious values of God's anointing hand. When we turn our lives over to Him, we also acknowledge this caring influence His healing promises have over us.

My life has had such a profound influence from my first encounter with God as a teenager. I was first challenged to accept Christ at a Billy Graham Crusade, so years later as an ex-Mormon Christian, I was moved to write to him, sharing my experiences.

After thanking him for his influence in my life as a teenager, I shared my experience in Mormonism and how God had faithfully led me back into His way again. I sent him a copy of a tract I had written in my efforts to reach Mormons still unaware of the contradictions between the Bible and the Mormon doctrines.

I shared the loss of my family with him and how the joys of my faith in Christ alone outweighed the suffering I had endured.

I had read Billy Graham's book entitled, Approaching Hoofbeats, and I knew that he was well informed on the subject of Mormon doctrine and vitally interested in seeing to it that people come to know the truth inherent with biblical Christianity.

My heart was lifted by a response that came to me from Mr. Graham's office, written by E.M. Engman. Among other things, it said:

> "...We rejoice that **the Lord was faithful and enlightened your understanding about Mormonism, bringing you out of that cult**. Surely losing your wife, family and friends must have been very difficult for you, but we do praise God that you had the courage to follow His leading, and you now feel that God is directing your life. May God bless you and prosper your ministry to others who have been **deceived by Mormonism**."

With such encouragement, building a new relationship and life in Christ has been a spiritual adventure of monumental proportions! To illustrate this, I remember my first confrontations with false Mormon teachings and also with lung and prostate cancer. In all three events, God's divine intervention was apparent when I began diligently searching the Scriptures and praying fervently. I could then realize God's prescription was not for my will but... "**His will be done** on earth as it is in heaven" (Matthew 6:10).

"Thus, whatever we pray for, whether it's healing or understanding, when our will is in harmony with His will, we will receive what we request 100% of the time. However, when we pray as Christ prayed,

'Nevertheless, not my will but thy will be done,' we can be reassured that even in sickness and tragedy '... **all** things work together for good to those who love God and are called according to His purpose.' (Romans 8:28)." (*The Bible Answer Book*, Hank Hanegraff)

Years before my life-saving experiences with cancer, I remember several Christian friends "diagnosing" me as a victim of Mormonism. Unfortunately, I paid little or no attention to them. I had been swept away with missionary's pride-building, precursory LDS Church bait (called "love-bombing" by other ex-Mormons). Before I could realize the tragic error of spiritual judgment I had made, I lapsed into the Mormon Church "busy-work," legalistic routines. It was really a very comfortable social culture that maintained a super-ego, spiritual coma in my life for the next 18 years.

Why didn't I apply the same investigative tools to becoming a Mormon as I did in being a cancer victim? Finding a cure was, of course, my main focus. I researched the different cancers including my own, attempting to locate the best doctors and hospitals available for treatment. Now this investigation along with my own prayers, those of my wife, family, friends and church members was carried out with great diligence and perseverance.

The Bible should have been my diagnostician before I made any commitment to join a church harboring beliefs that would have such disastrous consequences. I failed to realize how far off-base a church can be carried by doctrines of men. In retrospect, isn't one's eternal destiny worth the time and effort to first determine basic Christian doctrines before jumping into the "feel-good" deceptions of Mormonism? Unlike the *Book of Mormon*, the Bible can be trusted. Its fulfilled prophecies, archaeological discoveries, scientific accuracy, and the unity of all 40 to 50 inspired authors writing over a period of from 1,500 to 1,600 years is evidence of its validity. These were educated and uneducated men, from shepherds to statesmen, writing 66 books with a central theme portraying one perfect Savior as the Lord Jesus Christ!

The truth about Mormonism is cleverly hidden from new converts. Unless they study biblical references such as a "different" gospel men contrive or an angel (Moroni) preaching "any other gospel to you," the deception remains undetected (see Galatians 1:6-12).

"Let us experience and probe our ways and let us return to the Lord."   Lamentations 3:40

"Prove all things; hold fast that which is good." Thessalonians 5:21

To survive life, surely one needs to "prove all things and hold fast that which is good." By trusting in just good feelings (LDS "burning in the bosom"), it's the same as saying, "Don't tell me, doctor, I don't want to know! I feel fine…and I know the Church is true. All is well, all is well."[3]

It seems that cancer can't be cured, except by destroying it. It can't be prevented as it's a silent invader until it's "caught" or proven in time to be treatable.

To illustrate my dilemma in 2004, I set out to keep a doctor's appointment I had made for a physical. It had no special significance to me. I had no illness to complain about. In fact, my state of health might even be termed exuberant. Why did I even think about setting up this routine potpourri of "much-to-do about nothing?" (Now I realize God must have been prompting me!)

Most routine physicals don't include a chest x-ray, but my doctor just decided this was the time. "Not to worry," I thought to myself. I had quit smoking after a ten-year addiction beginning with my senior year in high school. I often thought I could never quit, but when I did, I couldn't stop bragging about my "heroic" achievement. I've always felt that quitting "cold turkey" after smoking one and a half packs a day for ten years was one of my major achievements in life.

Well, after 46 years of smokeless lungs, I couldn't believe my eyes when the doctor called me over to view my just-taken chest x-ray. He pointed to the upper left lobe and with hardly a ripple in his voice said, "There appears to be a 'shadow' right at this location about three centimeters in diameter."

I blurted the unthinkable, "Well, is it cancer?" Then, with a judicious bedside manner he explained, "We'll have to set up an appointment with a pulmonologist, who will take a biopsy to make sure exactly what it is."

Thus, I began a medical adventure from bronchoscopy to CAT scan to PET scan resulting in a diagnosis of operable stage II lung cancer.

---

[3] "Come, Come Ye Saints," LDS hymn.

But in no single instance could any of my doctors link smoking or any other carcinogen to this cancer. Indeed, my surgeon said he would guess the tumor to be about four or five years old. **And here I was, a cancer victim without knowing it!**

After removing the malignancy and following up with radiation and chemo, I'm in remission! Praising God for answering so many prayers on my behalf – and for each day we're given to glorify Him and not ourselves. I had walked around for five years with cancer in my body and didn't know it. I also walked around in Mormonism for 18 years without realizing it was a cult.

As a Mormon, I took such great pride in announcing that I didn't smoke, drink or use any harmful substance. I always felt such superiority over others by turning my coffee cup over in restaurants and ordering soft drinks while in a "drinking" crowd. Quitting smoking became such a prideful issue for me that it became my testimonial as one of the main reasons I became a Mormon.

Again, I mused how much my life as a Mormon had such an opposite effect on my spiritual relationship with Jesus Christ. I was lulled by the sense of pride I felt by living in accordance with the "Word of Wisdom." In fact, before I could be baptized and accepted as a new convert, I was required to abstain from using:

- Alcoholic beverages
- Coffee, tea or other "hot" drinks, or any hot or cold beverages with caffeine
- Tobacco or related drugs

> "And I, the Lord give unto them a promise that the destroying angel shall pass by them as the children of Israel, and not slay them. Amen."
>
> (*Doctrine and Covenants*, Section 89)

This "Word of Wisdom" commandment is also accepted by the church as a **<u>measuring rod</u>** to determine one's personal worthiness!

Well, obviously, Mormons who live by these standards will certainly reap the benefits of a healthy body. But does it take a "commandment" to do this? Does our worthiness protect us from the enemy? When good works are required to measure "letter of the law" requirements for salvation, Jesus has no part of the equation.

SALVATION/EXALTATION REQUIREMENTS OF THE MORMON CHURCH

(Works required of members whose ultimate goal is godhood!)

1. Absolute 100% perfection in all thoughts and deeds.

2. The work of Mormon baptism through priesthood authority only.

3. The work of Mormon Church membership and confirmation.

4. The work of ordination to the Mormon Priesthood held by male members.

5. The work of Mormon Temple requirements.

6. The work of Mormon temple washings and anointings.

7. The work of wearing temple undergarments with secret symbols for the rest of one's life.

8. The work of receiving a secret new name in the temple.

9. The work of the temple endowments (includes secret hand-shakes, their names, signs and penalties – taking oaths under penalty of death).

10. The work of being married for time and eternity in the temple (celestial marriage). There are no exceptions to this requirement.

11. The work of performing temple work for the dead. (Temple workers are called "saviors on Mt. Zion.") Baptism, endow-ments, and sealings are all performed by proxy on behalf of members' kindred dead.

12. The work of tithing to only the Mormon Church.

13. The work of not drinking tea, coffee, alcoholic beverages, or using tobacco.

14. The work of having as many children as possible considering one's situation.

15. The work of following "the living prophet and his counselors – follow them and be blessed; reject them and suffer." President Ezra Taft Benson

BIBLICAL CHRISTIANITY is clear and to the point; it is in direct conflict with the false doctrines of Joseph Smith's Mormon illusion of Christianity – a counterfeit and a cult that uses a façade of Christian terms.

Read the following Bible verses and compare them with the shadowy world of Joseph's "restoration" of "the gospel in all its fullness"...a gospel of work unrelated to Jesus' atonement of dying for ALL our sins. SALVATION BY FAITH...NOT WORKS.

Ephesians 2:8, 9	John 3:15, 16
Galatians 2:16	John 6:47
Romans 3:26-28	Romans 1:16 – 3:22, 3:30 – 10:9-11, 13
Galatians 3:22-26	II Timothy 3:15
Romans 3:20-23	Romans 4:6-9 – 5:1, 2 – 10:4
Philippians 3:9	John 11:25, 26
Galatians 3:10-12	Galatians 2:21
Galatians 4:4, 5	I John 5: 11-13
Titus 3:4-7	Romans 6:23
Galatians 5:1-6	John 5:24
Romans 10:1-13	

From the above, the Bible definitely teaches that one is fully and totally saved of ALL SINS only by a faith in Jesus that has absolutely nothing to do with good works. Christians do good works because of Jesus' unconditional (Romans 8:1) love. In a personal relationship with Jesus, we follow Him alone as He dwells in us. Good works become the result of that relationship!

Isaiah 64:6: "For all of us have become like one who is unclean, and all our righteous deeds (works) are like filthy rags."

JUST A FEW WORKS, RULES AND REGULATIONS!

1. "Laughter on the Sabbath Day is expressly curtailed." *Doctrine & Covenants* 59:15

2. "While studying, Elders were commanded to abstain from all laughter." *D&C* 88:120

3. "Idle words, jesting, and light speeches" are beneath "the dignity of the called and chosen of God." *Mormon Doctrine*, pg. 373

4. "Cursings may be administered by the power and authority of priesthood." *D&C* 124:93

5. "Those who waste time in doing nothing commit the grievous sin of idleness." *MD*, pg. 372

6. Non-member parents of a Mormon are not permitted to attend the temple wedding of their son or daughter. Temple attendance requires membership and "worthiness" of the participant.

7. "When Mormon leaders speak, the thinking has been done. When they point the way, there is no other way which is safe." *Improvement Era* – June, 1945, p. 354

8. The true test of truth for Mormons is based on having "good feelings" or a "burning in the bosom" after praying about it. The prophet of the Mormon Church has absolute authority over the membership and is considered infallible as "God's mouthpiece." *MD*, pg. 606 – *D&C* 9:8

9. Missionaries' hair length is strictly monitored – no moustaches or beards.

10. Missionaries must wear white shirts and ties, dark suits, dress shoes. Identification badges must be worn on the left.

11. Temple patrons are warned never to speak of temple activities outside the temple. Oaths are taken to keep everything secret. Mormons (over 70%) have no idea what goes on inside a Mormon Temple!

12. Non-conforming dress and appearance are criticized. At Brigham Young University, dress codes are strictly enforced.

13. One must only use the right hand to take the bread and **water** used as the Mormon communion elements.

14. If any body part is exposed to the air during baptism, the ordinance must be repeated. Baptism by immersion is a requirement for salvation/exaltation.

15. If any "sacrament prayer" is not offered word-for-word, no matter how slight the error, it must be repeated.

16. Standing in church to sing hymns is not an acceptable practice.

17. No recreational activities are permitted on Sundays.

18. It is a direct commandment of God to attend "Sacrament Meetings" on Sunday.

19. Failure to tithe regularly brings condemnation of God.

20. Blessings come by personal achievement of maintaining one's "worthiness" and adherence to church doctrines/policies.

CHAPTER TEN

Recovery, One Step at a Time

Of course there are many programs in the Mormon Church that provide opportunities for personal involvement. One has to admire how much responsibility is offered to the lay membership. But one must realize that there is far more to contemplate in choosing a church than social activities, spiritual-worthiness, and good-works requirements.

If I had applied the same care I used in choosing a surgeon and a hospital as I should have made in choosing a Christian church, I would never have entertained the thought of becoming a Mormon. There are many medical choices to make that are offered to cancer patients. Which is the best? Whose opinion do you take? When one's life is on the line, there's no room for slip-up. I don't know of anyone who makes this decision casually. So why do people spend so little time investigating the doctrines of many pseudo-Christian churches before making a commitment that has eternal consequences? Years ago, I still remember hearing the admonition of my high school auto shop teacher:

"When all else fails, read the directions!"

If I had taken his advice to heart, reading and studying the Bible would have been a spiritual foundation to help me avoid being deceived by false doctrines or false prophets. Yes! Indeed, the Bible is truly God's ownership manual for our life's journey. His Word does not return void (Isaiah 55:11)!

"Rejoice always; pray without ceasing; in everything give
thanks; for this is God's will for you in Christ Jesus."

I Thess. 5:16-18

Give thanks in **everything**? Yes, that's what Scripture tells us.

As I look back in time, I think how many times God has applied His promises to my life's problems. One in particular stands out above all the rest:

> "And we know that God causes all things to work together for good, to those who love God, to those who are called according to His purpose."   Romans 8:28

Everyone makes poor choices in life...they may be downright stupid, ill-advised, self-centered, egotistical, irrational or illogical ones to say the least. But, in all those periods of spurious understanding, **God will cause all things to work together for good to those who love Him and are called accordingly to His purpose.** Where or when does one realize that God is so important?

> ".... because that which is known about God is evident within them; for God made it evident to them...**His invisible attributes, His eternal power and divine nature have been clearly seen, being understood through what has been made**, so that they are without excuse."   Romans 1:19, 20

If we go through life just accepting its grandeur and complexity without much thought, we're not much higher than mere animal life. How much time do people spend admiring God's creations such as a beautiful sunset or majestic cloud formations? How can people possibly deal with the "rain" that falls on both the "righteous and the unrighteous" (Matthew 5:45) if they fail to acknowledge their Creator?

God calls each of us, independent of church affiliation or not, to love Him above all else.

> "You shall love the Lord your God with all your heart, with all your soul, and with all your mind. This is the first and great commandment."   Matthew 22:37, 38

The Bible - Step By Step

I believe God wants, above all else, to enjoy a relationship with each of us. The spiritual concepts behind each of the Twelve Steps programs appear throughout the Bible. Isn't it interesting how many non-Christian organizations there are utilizing this program as the very best approach to deal with many obsessive dependencies. Certainly Mormonism, as well, fits this category!

In our hour of greatest need for God's healing touch, what better time to realize God's plan for the spiritual awareness of His presence and **unconditional love.**

Take this time, right now, to realize how much God loves you. Read aloud His Word as an exercise in the Twelve Steps. There are many Scriptures that back up each of these twelve attitudes, both spiritually and physically, in pointing the way to God's "supervision" in your life for victorious living and recovery from the ills of this world. It's time well spent, and it works!

> **"But be doers of the word, not hearers only."**   James 1:22

Then they said to Him "What shall we do, that we may work the works of God?"

Jesus answered,

> **"This is the work of God, that you believe** in Him whom He Sent."
> John 6:29

> "...work out your own salvation with fear and trembling;
> for it is God who works in you both to will and to do for
> His good pleasure."   Philippians 2:12, 13

> "And take the helmet of salvation, and the sword of the Spirit,
> **which is the word of God**; praying always with all prayer and
> supplication in the Spirit..."   Ephesians 6:17, 18

> "Let us therefore draw near with confidence to the throne of
> grace, that we may receive mercy and may find grace to help
> in the time of need."   Hebrews 4:15

> "Order my steps in thy word; and let not any iniquity have
> dominion over me."   Psalm 119:133

The spiritual concepts behind the Twelve Steps appear through-out the Bible. Here is a small sampling of passages as quoted from the Alochol Anonymous (AA) tracts that support each "Step." As you read through them, think of them less as "proof texts" and more as "connecting links" between the Steps and the Scriptures, between recovery and faith.

Step One

We admitted we were powerless over the effects of our separation from God.

Psalms 6:6-10; 34:17-18	Matthew 9:36
Romans 7:15-20	Proverbs 28:25-26
1 Corinthians 8:2	Isaiah 38:12-13
2 Corinthians 12:9-10	

Step Two

Came to believe that only God could restore us to personal wholeness.

Deuteronomy 33:27	Luke 5:31; 15:17
Job 6:8	John 3:16
Psalms 63:1; 91:1	**Romans 8:38-39**
Isaiah 41:10; 61:10	2 Corinthians 1:9; 3:5
Jeremiah 30:17	**Philippians 2:13; 4:19**
Ezekiel 18:31	Hebrews 11:6
Mark 5:15; 9:23-24; 10:51	I Peter 5:7

Step Three

Made a decision to turn our will and our lives over to the care of God.

Deuteronomy 30:19-20	Lamentations 3:26
Psalms 40:1-2 ; 118:8-9	Matthew 4:18-22; 7:7; 11:28-30
Proverbs 3:5-6; 16:3; 18:10	Mark 12:30
Isaiah 40:31; 55:1	Galatians 2:20
Jeremiah 17:14	Philippians 2:12-13

Step Four

Made a searching and fearless inventory of ourselves.

Psalm 4:4	John 14:1
Proverbs 27:12	I Corinthians 13:5-6
Jeremiah 17:9-10	Ephesians 4:31
Lamentations 3:40	Colossians 3:5-8
Joel 2:12-13	James 1:19-21; 3:14-16
Micah 6:8	2 Peter 1:5-7
Matthew 26:41	1 John 1:8-9

Step Five

Admitted to God, to ourselves, and to another human being the exact nature of our wrongs.

Psalms 32:3-5; 51:17; 55:22	Luke 15:18-19
Proverbs 18:24; 27:17	Romans 3:23; 14:12
Isaiah 44:22	Ephesians 1:7-8
Jeremiah 14:20	**James 4:7-8; 5:16**
Daniel 9:4	I John 1:8-9; 2:1-2

Step Six

Were entirely ready to have God remove all these defects of character.

Psalm 119:10-12; 139:23-24	Philippians 3:12-14
Proverbs 3:24	I Thessalonians 5:23-24
Lamentations 3:19-22	Hebrews 9:14
Ezekiel 36:25	**James 4:10**
John 15:7	I Peter 1:13-14
Romans 6:11-12	I John 5:14

Step Seven

Humbly asked him to remove our shortcomings.

Psalm 25:8-11; 34:7; 51:1-2, 10-12	**John 15:2**
Isaiah 41:13	Acts 3:19
Ezekiel 36:25-26	Romans 4:20-21; 8:1-2
Matthew 21:22; 23:12	James 4:6-8
Mark 11:24	I John 1:9; 5:15

Step Eight

Made a list of all persons we had harmed and became willing to make amends to them all.

Deuteronomy 31:6	Luke 6:27-31, 37-38; 19:8
Proverbs 25:9-10	Romans 2:1; 15:1-3
Jeremiah 35:15	Ephesians 4:32
Matthew 6:14-15; 7:3-5	I John 4:11-12
Mark 11:25	

Step Nine

Made direct amends to such people wherever possible, except when to do so would injure them or others.

Leviticus 19:17-18   Ephesians 4:25-28

Ezekiel 33:15-16   Philippians 2:3-4, 14-15

Matthew 5:23-26; 43-45   Colossians 3:12-13

Luke 6:31-36   I John 2:9-10; 4:19-21

Romans 12:14-21; 13:8; 14:13

Step Ten

Continued to take personal inventory and when we were wrong promptly admitted it.

Psalms 19:12;   **I Corinthians 10:12**
34:12; 139:23-24

Proverbs 14:29-30; 21:2   2 Corinthians 3:5

Ezekiel 33:14-16   James 1:23-25

Mark 14:38   I John 1:7

Luke 6:27-31; 6:41-42   Jude 24-25

Romans 12:3   Ephesians 4:22-24; 5:15-16

Step Eleven

Sought through prayer and meditation to improve our conscious contact with God, praying only for knowledge of His will for us and the power to carry that out.

Psalm 1:1-3; 16:7-8;   Matthew 6:6, 9-13; 7:7
25:4-5; 37:7-9;
88:9; 119:105-106   Mark 11:24

Proverbs 3:5-6; 16:20   Luke 11:9-10

Isaiah 26:3-4; 30:21   Romans 8:26

Lamentations 3:25-26   Philippians 4:6

Hosea 6:3   Colossians 1:10; 3:16

Step Twelve

Having had a spiritual awakening as the result of these steps, we tried to carry this message to others, and to practice these principles in all our affairs.

Psalm 71:15-18; 78:1-8	**I John 1:7**
Ecclesiastes 4:5-11	Galatians 6:1
Isaiah 38:10-20	Ephesians 5:1-2
Matthew 25:40; 28:19-20	Philippians 4:8-9
Mark 5:19	Colossians 4:5-6
Luke 8:16-18; 14:12-14	2 Timothy 4:2
Romans 8:1-2; 12:1-2	Hebrews 13:15-16
2 Corinthians 5:17-20	I Peter 4:8-11

In 2 Corinthians 13:5, 6, Paul exhorts us to "Examine yourselves as to whether you are in the faith. Test yourselves. Do you know yourselves, that Jesus Christ is in you? - unless indeed you are disqualified. But I trust that you will know that we are not disqualified."

Of course, when Jesus "is in you" by your decision to receive His gift of salvation, you have maximum security in Him (John 1: 12, 13).

Jesus never left me. I left Him for 18 years of being deceived, but He prevailed! His truth and Spirit kept prodding me to question LDS "authority." Even limited Biblical knowledge helped me realize Mormon error!

CHAPTER ELEVEN

Choosing Life

"I have set before you life and death, blessing and cursing;
therefore choose life, that both of you and your descendants
may live; that you may love the Lord your God, that you may
obey His voice, and that you may cling to Him..."

Deuteronomy 30:19, 20

The Bible offers our creator's utmost design for righteous and joyous living:

Jesus said, "I have come that they may have life, and that they
may have it more abundantly!"   John 10:10

"...and you will find Him if you seek Him with all your heart
and with all your soul."   Deuteronomy 4:2

God has a plan for each of us, but not wanting to force His way upon us we must make the decision to seek Him first.

How belligerent and gullible we as humans have become "to exchange the truth of God for a lie, and worshipped and served the creature rather than the Creator..." Romans 1:25.

Jamie Foxx, who portrayed Ray Charles in the movie, **Ray**, was playing the piano along with the virtuoso one day while shooting the film. He was scolded by the famous jazz musician for hitting just one wrong note. Since that time, Jamie has made a commitment to himself to "see" the piano keys as a metaphor for the care we should take in not hitting the wrong notes of life's multiple choices. As an accomplished pianist, it's just one slip that can ruin a performance, no matter how perfect the rest of the composition is played. So it is with life...just one careless choice without **His Way** can result in tragedy.

God wants us to **seek Him first!** He has provided us a most extravagant banquet of His counsel that far surpasses any of man's deviations.

Psalm 119 is a tribute to the overwhelming power inherent in His Word. Consider the varied synonyms this Psalm uses to emphasize the qualifying references to the **Word of God**:

The law of the Lord

His testimonies

His way

His precepts

His statues

His commandments

His judgments

His ordinances

My 'hiding place'

My 'shield'

My 'hope'

My 'understanding'

My 'delights'

His 'righteousness'

"Through <u>Your precepts</u> I get understanding;
Therefore, I hate every false way.
<u>*Your word*</u> *is a lamp to my feet*
And a light to my path."
Psalm 119: 104, 105

The word "way" is also used as a synonym for all these terms found in Psalm 119. Please read it again!

There are over 150 references to the synonyms for God's Word in Psalm 119! The Scofield Study Bible says, "This Psalm, born of love for the law of God, extols the beauties and excellences of the written Word of God in a way found nowhere else in the Bible."

The healing benefits of knowing God's Word and having firsthand experience of using its counsel is one of life's most rewarding experiences. Examine some of God's promises and consider what a treasure we have at our fingertips:

> "<u>Your word I have hidden in my heart</u>, that I might not sin against You." "Your word is a lamp to my feet and a light for my path." Psalm 119:11,105

> "<u>I am not ashamed of the gospel</u>, because it is the power of God for the salvation to everyone who believes." Romans 1:16

> "For <u>these commands are a lamp, this teaching is a light</u> and the corrections of discipline are the way of life." Proverbs 6:23

"The **unfolding of your words gives light**; it gives understanding to the simple." Psalm 119:130

"**For the Word of God is living and active**. Sharper than any double-edged sword, it penetrates even to the dividing of soul and spirit, joints and marrow; it judges the thoughts and attitudes of the heart." Hebrews 4:12

"Consequently, **faith comes from hearing the message**, and the **message is heard through the Word of Christ**." Romans 10:17

"But **be doers of the Word**, and not hearers only, deceiving yourselves. For if anyone is a hearer of the Word and not a doer, he is **like a man observing his natural face in a mirror**; for he observes himself, goes away, and immediately **forgets what kind of man he was**." James 1:22-24

"**All scripture is given by inspiration of God**, and is profitable **for doctrine**, for **reproof**, for **correction**, for **instruction** in righteousness, that the man of God may be complete, **thoroughly equipped for every good work**." 2 Timothy 3:15-17

My surviving cancer and Mormonism are not expressions of opposite inclinations. They incorporate two very distinct and parallel battles for survival of body and soul. They are alike in so many ways!

To confront either of these worldly bastions of human affliction and domination, God's Word has been my shield and fortress. In both maladies there has been the enemy's underlying attack to extinguish the Holy Spirit that has counseled me through so many of life's misadventures, poor choices, and naive pursuits.

I marvel at God's perseverance to never give up on me, and all He wants in return is for us to love Him with an unwavering faith and belief in Him alone. That belief is inherent with knowing Him as the Living "Word," Jesus, as described in John 1:1-5 which expresses the Deity of Jesus Christ. The detour I took into the Mormon Church as an inexperienced Christian seemed permanent. However, even after 18 years, my early Bible training through just hearing sermons and Sunday School class lessons made a difference by having His Word *"hidden in my heart that I might not sin against you"* Psalm 119:11. My decision to give my heart to the Lord as a junior high school student had a significant impact on my life as a Mormon. It made it impossible for me to remain faithful to doctrines I inherently knew to be false.

I couldn't understand the loyalty of my wife and many other personal church friends to LDS teaching, which they also questioned and could not adequately defend.

God's Word is life personified! It's the final authoritative, infallible, powerful and persuasive voice of our creator reaching out to every human being to "Trust in the Lord with all your heart, and lean not on your own understanding; in all your ways acknowledge Him, and **He shall direct your paths.**" Proverbs 3:5,6

What does the Bible say we must do to merit such a "wonderful counselor" (Isaiah 9:6) and to be saved from our sins and unrighteousness? Achieve the status of "worthy Mormons" by our accomplishments of good works? Follow the myriad lists of do's and don'ts prescribed by the Mormon hierarchy of prophets and apostles and earn the right to become "gods?"

How blatant and blasphemous can men's pride extend to presume that godhood may be achieved by following the dictates of the "prophet" Joseph Smith? Just read what he wrote as a "divine revelation from God," or was it from that old deceiver, the "god of this world" who "blinded the minds of them which believe not...?" (II Corinthians 4:4)

Joseph Smith said:

> "And as pertaining to the new and everlasting covenant (temple marriage), it was instituted for the fullness of My glory; and he that receiveth a fullness thereof **must and shall abide the law,** or he shall be damned, saith the Lord God..."
>
> **Then shall they be gods,** because they have no end; therefore shall they be from everlasting to everlasting, because they continue; then shall they be above all, because **they have all power, and the angels are subject unto them.**
>
> "Verily, verily, I say unto you, except you **abide my law, ye cannot attain to this glory.**" Joseph Smith Jr.
> *Doctrine and Covenants* 132:6, 20, 21
>
> "From this revelation, it will be seen that **men can become Gods** and enjoy a 'fullness and a continuation of the seeds forever and ever'..." Mormon Apostle, L. Richards
> (*A Marvelous Work and a Wonder*), p. 312,313

If the 10,000,000+ members of the Church of "Jesus Christ" of Latter-Day Saints would devote their lives to a one-on-one relationship with the real Jesus and the Bible, I'm sure they would realize the deception of their doctrines, priesthoods, prophets and apostles as I did by just highlighting the **hundreds** of biblical Scriptures that are diametrically opposed to Mormon theology. (see "A Few Comparison Notes" in Epilogue)

> **"For there is one God and <u>one</u> Mediator between God and**
> **men, the man Christ Jesus."** I Timothy 2:5

God's Word is the only biblical authoritative record in existence that proves Jesus Christ is exactly who He claimed to be. God's Word removes all doubt; it is His Way that removes the roadblocks and barricades to a life-sustaining faith that surmounts all obstacles.

Without Jesus in my life, I would never have survived 18 years of Joseph Smith's "different gospel," which the apostle Paul warns is a perversion of the gospel of Christ, Galatians 1:6,7. "But even if we, or an angel from heaven, (the LDS angel, Moroni) **preach any other gospel to you than what we have preached to you, let him be accursed."** Galatians 1:8

I reflect on those 18 years of Mormon spiritual blindness with empathy for those who are so caught up in this counterfeit of Christianity that dominated my thinking so fervently. And so I feel I must share that passage of my life with as many as possible in thankfulness and praise for His gift of a new life in Christ.

The pseudo-Christian cults can be very respectable churches from an outsider's point of view. One must be alert to the subtle emotional influences used to circumvent false doctrinal foundations as they creep into seemingly orthodox Christian teaching. A charismatic leader or "prophet" has those same qualities as some of our most beloved and adored entertainers and politicians. What they say can also have much influence on the electorate and yet, their credentials for determining our standards of government are nil.

Our wisdom is determined by how we apply God's Word to our lives. "We know also that the **Son of God has come and has given us understanding**, so **that we may know Him who is true**. And we are in Him who is true – even in His Son Jesus Christ. He is the true God and eternal life." 1 John 5:20

If we "...receive God's Word with all readiness of mind, and search the Scriptures daily, whether those things were so" Acts 17:11, we will be able to detect the wolves in sheep's clothing with little difficulty. Our safeguard against the cults that deceive is the certainty we have in the Bible, that God Himself is a "bulwark never failing"![4]

"The Word" is also a designation for Jesus:

"In the beginning was the Word, and the Word was with God and the Word was God." John 1:1

"And the Word became flesh and dwelt among us, and we beheld His glory, the glory as of the only begotten of the Father, full of grace and truth." John 1:14

Jesus is literally the embodiment of God's divine wisdom and collective thought. He is the personification of all God stands for as:

1.	Advocate	1 John 2:1
2.	Author of eternal salvation	Hebrews 5:9
3.	Counselor	Isaiah 9:6
4.	Deliverer	Romans 11:26
5.	God	Isaiah 40:9; John 20:28; 1 John 5:20
6.	High Priest, our only	Hebrews 4:14; 5:10
7.	King of Kings	1 Timothy 6:15; Revelation 17:14; 19:16
8.	Lord God Almighty	Revelation 15:3
9.	Lord of Lords	1 Timothy 6:15; Revelation 17:14; 19:16
10.	Mediator	1 Timothy 2:5; Hebrews 12:24
11.	Mighty God	Isaiah 9:6

---

[4]Hymn: "A Mighty Fortress," Martin Luther.

12. Prophet	Deuteronomy 18:15; Luke 24:19
13. Redeemer	Job 19:25; Isaiah 59:20
14. Savior	Luke 2:11; Acts 5:31

He is sufficient! Jesus is Lord!

If your Christian commitment is connected to a church system of good works, earned salvation, a progressive exaltation of self; or, to ignore sin by denying its existence, etc., you're trying to be in charge of your own eternal destiny!

As a Mormon, I was in a spiritual bondage to a religious system devised by one man, Joseph Smith. His imagined "restoration" of the church that was established by Jesus Christ is a sacrilege of Jesus' redemption of our sins by His shed blood. No additional work by anyone is required! Jesus' last words, "It is finished," is His seal of authority over any false prophet who would usurp God's plan of salvation.

When I received Jesus alone to take His rightful place as the Lord of my life, I was following His plan:

> "That if you confess with your mouth the Lord Jesus and believe in your heart that God raised Him from the dead, you will be saved. For with the heart one believes unto righteousness, and with the mouth confession is made unto salvation."
>
> Romans 10:9-10

Dear Reader, If you've never submitted your life to Jesus and God's Word, how will you ever really know Him as Lord and Savior? With this prayer, let God recognize the true intent of your heart...

Dear God, *I know that my sins have separated me from you. So I thank you for sending your Son, Jesus Christ, to die in my place. Deliver me from the deceptions of false prophets so that your Word prevails in my life and* **all** *my sins are nailed to the cross. Please forgive my sins. Come into my life, dear Jesus, and direct my life. Thank you for your gift of eternal life in Christ Jesus. Amen*

> "And do not be conformed to the world, **but be transformed by the renewing of your mind, that you may prove what is that good and acceptable and perfect will of God**."
>
> Romans 12:2

Above all, "prove all things; hold fast that which is good!"

1 Thess. 5:21

Dear Jesus, Your blessed gift of salvation and eternal life is complete. According to your Word, Mormonism no longer has any hold on my life. Its darkness has succumbed to your marvelous light! Indeed, You've delivered me from the chains of legalism and Your Truth has made me free. I praise your blessed name forever, "My Lord and my God!"[5]

Tom Hall

---

[5]John 20:28

A FEW OUTRAGEOUS MORMON BELIEFS

Copied from *MORMON DOCTRINE* by LDS Apostle, Bruce McConkie
(An encyclopedia-type compendium of actual Mormon doctrines)

I. Godhood

p. 321   *"... you have got to learn how to be gods yourselves..."*

"God himself was once as we are now, and is an exalted man..."

Joseph Smith, founder of the LDS Church

p. 516   *"An exalted and glorified Man of Holiness could not be a Father (God) unless a Woman of like glory, perfection, and holiness was associated with him as a Mother."*   Joseph Smith

p. 321   *"... he (God) was once a man like us; yea, that God himself, the Father of us all, dwelt on an earth, the same as Jesus Christ himself did...*   Joseph Smith

p. 516   *"(All men)...are also the offspring of an Eternal Mother."*

II. Godhood & The Mormon Church

The Church of Jesus Christ of Latter-Day Saints, *a.k.a.* *"LDS"*

p. 134   "Those who join the (only) true Church (LDS) and keep their covenants <u>gain salvation</u> in the celestial kingdom of God."

p. 20   "...*the* Garden of Eden was located in what is known to us as the land of Zion, an area which <u>Jackson County</u>, <u>Missouri</u> is the center place."

pg. 171   "When the Father and the Son appeared to Joseph Smith... he was told to 'join none of them (other churches) for they were all wrong... all their creeds were an abomination in his sight.' "

p. 671   "One of the untrue doctrines found in modern Chris-
           tendom (all Christian churches) is the concept that
           man can gain salvation by grace alone and without
           obedience. (works) This soul-destroying doctrine…"

III. The *Book of Mormon* or The Bible ?

p. 82   The Bible has many omissions and errors.
           "…they have taken away from the gospel of the Lamb
           many parts which are plain and most precious;"
                                  Book of Mormon I Nephi 13:26

p. 99   "I told the brethren that the Book of Mormon was
           the most correct of any book on earth, and the
           keystone of our religion…"   Joseph Smith

p. 383   "…the Prophet (Joseph Smith) corrected, revised,
           altered, added to, and deleted from the King James
           Version of the Bible to form what is now commonly
           referred to as the Inspired Version of the Bible."
           (This Joseph Smith translation is available as a
           resource, but the KJV Bible is the only "authorized"
           LDS translation. All Mormon "prophets" and their
           "revelations" supersede scripture!)

p. 608   "Inspired statements (of LDS prophets) are scripture
           and should be accepted as such."
                                  Doctrine & Covenants 68:4

p. 616   "The Book of Mormon explains why Lamanites
           (Blacks) received dark skins and a degenerate status."
                                  (*BM*) 2 Nephi 5: 21-23

p. 527   (The Mormon [LDS] Church prohibited Blacks from
           holding their priesthood until 1978 when the prophet
           had a "revelation" to change the doctrine.)

p. 648   "Wherefore, because that you have a Bible, you
           need not suppose that it contains all my words;
           neither need you suppose that I have not caused
           more to be written."   (*BM*) 2 Nephi 29: 7-10

IV. The LDS Jesus

p. 214 — The Mormon "Jesus" is considered to be our *Elder Brother.* "Since all men are the personal spirit children of the Father, and since Christ was the Firstborn spirit offspring, it follows that he is the Elder Brother of all men."

p. 193 — In a Mormon pre-existence, Jesus and Lucifer are considered <u>spirit brothers</u>: "Satan (Lucifer) offered (to a council of the Gods) to come into the world as the Son of God and be the Redeemer." "Christ said, in effect: 'Here am I. Send me; I will be thy son...' "

p. 92, 93 — "Man may commit certain grievous sins - *according to his light and knowledge* - that will place him beyond the reach of the atoning Blood of Christ." - "...there are some serious sins for which the cleansing (blood atonement) of Christ does not operate, and the law of God is that men must then have their own blood shed to atone for their sins."

p. 677 — "Those (LDS temple workers) who perform, vicariously, for others—meaning for those who have died without a knowledge of the gospel, *the saving ordinances* which they cannot perform for themselves, are called <u>saviors</u> on Mt. Zion."

p. 319 — "God the Father (Elohim) is a glorified and perfected Man, a Personage *of flesh and bones,* in which a tangible body and eternal spirit is housed."

P. 130 — "(Jesus)... is the Son of God the Father, and as such is a separate and distinct personage from the Father... the Father authorizes him <u>to speak in the first person as though he were the Father.</u>"

p. 581   "(prayers)… are to be addressed (only) to the Father (Elohim); they should always be made (ended) in the name of Jesus Christ.

p. 339   "The grace (of Jesus Christ) is granted to men proportionately as they conform to the standards (works) of personal righteousness that are part of the gospel plan."

p. 677   *"SAVIORS OF MEN* : By preaching the gospel of (Mormon) salvation to the world, the (LDS) saints become the *saviors of men."*   V. Joseph Smith

V. Joseph Smith

p. 396   "Since <u>the keys of salvation were restored to the Prophet</u>, (Joseph Smith) it is in and through and because of his Latter-Day mission that the <u>full redemptive power of the Lord</u> has again become available to men. It is because the Lord called Joseph Smith that salvation is again available to men."

p. 396   *"Joseph Smith, the Prophet and Seer of the Lord, has done more, save Jesus only, for the salvation of men in this world than any other man that lived in it."*
           (D&C 135:3)

p. 592   "The President of the Church (All LDS presidents are "prophets") is the mouthpiece of God on earth… *'For his word ye shall receive, as if from mine own mouth, in all patience and faith.'* "   *(D&C* 21:4,5)

p. 334   "The true gospel of Jesus Christ was restored to earth in the last days through the instrumentality of Joseph Smith. It is found <u>only</u> in *The Church of Jesus Christ of Latter-Day Saints."*

By reading these referenced Mormon beliefs, it is apparent the Mormon Jesus has nothing in common with the historic Jesus of the Bible! LDS missionaries always say they believe their name, *The Church of Jesus Christ of Latter-Day Saints* (Mormon), indicates they are a Christian church... What do you think?

Christian Outreach to LDS

P.O. Box 493, San Juan Capistrano, CA 92693
e-mail: halltrumpet@yahoo.com | website: mormonchronicles.com

EVALUATING INFORMATION

Dear Reader,

It is my fervent prayer that this book is a helpful resource tool when confronted with Mormon missionaries or those who believe the LDS Church is a Christian church and not a cult. Mormons have been led to the Lord of biblical Christianity by reading exactly what I experienced before, during and after my 18 years as a member, elder, and Mormon Temple initiate.

Please fill out this page and mail to the address below. You are also invited to order five or more copies of *Mormon Chronicles of Deception* to reach out to your LDS friends and their allies. To thank you, a free copy of the DVD, *Jesus Christ / Joseph Smith*, will be mailed to you on request.

In His Love and His Word,
Tom Hall

Name
_____

Address
_____

City   State   Zip
_____

Phone
_____

___Please send _____copies   ___Send free copy of Jesus
of this book " $5.00 each   Christ/ Joseph Smith CD
(discount rate).

_____Check Number

Comments for constructive evaluation?

_____

_____

_____

_____

What did you find most helpful about this book?

_____

_____

_____

_____

_____

MAIL TO:
Tom Hall
Christian Outreach to LDS
P.O. Box 493
San Juan Capistrano, CA 92693

Email: halltrumpet@yahoo.com
Website: www.mormonchronicles.com